"I've seen many careers stalled or de
ingly subtle behaviors that sabotage l
'self-diagnose' your blind spots and understand the impact of perceptions on
your career success."

—**Marcia Silverberg**, Vice President, Chief Human Resources Officer
Ascension Health, HR Strategic Initiatives and System Office

"There are few things more valuable or fragile than your reputation. But too
many of us either lack the courage to ask what others really think or aren't
willing to consciously develop virtuous habits that will shape how others see
us. This book will help you see yourself through the eyes of others, so you can
become the person you were meant to be."

—**Jeffrey Sandefer**, Founder, Acton School of Business
Named by *Business Week* as one of the top
Entrepreneurship Professors in the United States

"This book gives a vivid description of the many ways leaders undermine
their own reputations and careers. It will help you see yourself 'warts and all.'
More importantly, in what feels like a very personal coaching session, Sara
Canaday then gives you very candid and caring advice for how to succeed. An
immensely practical and useful guide."

—**Mette Norgaard,** Consultant and Co-Author of the *New York Times*
and *Wall Street Journal* Best Seller, *"TouchPoints"*

"One of the truisms of business is that 'perception is reality.' In ***You —
According to Them,*** Author Sara Canaday takes this concept from the business
level to the personal level. Buying this book and reading it will definitely help
you. It's a book you will want to mark up and make personal notes in, and
you can use it to build your own action plan for self-improvement."

—**George Lucas, Ph.D.**, Executive Vice President, U.S. Learning Inc.
Co-Author of the *New York Times* Best Seller, *"The One Minute Negotiator"*

"Sara Canaday is really on to something here. She understands the issues
leaders face and offers useful, practical advice to advance not only your career
but your life."

—**Sylvia Acevedo**, CEO, CommuniCard LLC
Commissioner, President's Advisory Commission
on Educational Excellence for Hispanics

"The top-performing leaders I studied were all adept at using their reputations to lead more effectively. They had to learn those skills on their own, just like you did, until Sara Canaday wrote *You — According to Them*. Read this book to find out how you can assess your own reputation and use what you learn to achieve all the success you deserve."

—**Wally Bock**, Leadership Expert, Author and Speaker

"This powerful book is packed full of actual case studies and brilliant strategies to help advance your career. Sara's insights are unique and revealing, bringing vision and clarity to overcoming blind spots and understanding others' perceptions of you. Through this book, Sara masterfully coaches you toward adopting behaviors that will positively impact your career and help you achieve greater success."

—**Sherry Maysonave**, President, Empowerment Enterprises
Author of *"Casual Power"*

"*You — According to Them* is a must-read for anyone serious about improving the perceived value of their personal brand. It will help readers understand the power of personal reputation and how others' perceptions can impact their ability to compete in the marketplace. Sara's clear writing style and helpful 'fast fixes' make it easy for readers to evaluate their own reputations, take action to elevate them, and accelerate their own journeys towards success."

—**Dr. Rich Handley**, President & Founder, EQ University

"Sara Canaday's *You — According to Them* hits the nail right on the head. Want to have a great company with customers who love you and keep coming back? Start on the inside. Help your leaders fix their blind spots, and they'll build the kind of workplace where customer-facing employees can be their best."

—**Jill Griffin**, International Speaker and Corporate Advisor
Author of Business Best Seller,
"Customer Loyalty: How To Earn It, How To Keep It"

YOU
ACCORDING TO THEM

Uncovering the blind spots that impact
your reputation and your career

SARA CANADAY

You — According to Them
By Sara Canaday
T&C Press

Published by T&C Press, Austin, TX
Copyright © 2012 Sara Canaday.
All rights reserved.

Applied Self-Awareness is a trademark of Sara Canaday & Associates.

Editor: Susan Priddy
Index: Nancy Humphreys
Cover and Interior Design: Highwire Creative

Library of Congress Control Number: 2012935759

Canaday, Sara
You — According to Them: Uncovering the blind spots that impact your reputation and your career / Sara Canaday. – 1st ed.

ISBN: 978-0-9846591-1-1

Includes index.

Printed in the United States of America

Disclaimer: The names in the stories have been changed in this book at author's discretion or the participants' request.

ATTENTION CORPORATIONS, UNIVERSITIES, COLLEGES AND PROFESSIONAL ORGANIZATIONS: Quantity discounts are available on bulk purchases of this book for large groups, sales promotions, as gifts, or for educational purposes. Special books or book excerpts can also be created to fit specific needs. For information, please contact: info@youaccordingtothem.com

www.YouAccordingToThem.com
www.SaraCanaday.com

ACKNOWLEDGMENTS

Heartfelt and sincere gratitude to my development editor Susan Priddy, without whom this book would not have been written and whose relentless support, encouragement, sense of humor, and wisdom helped me develop a more comprehensive and relatable book. Her commitment to this book and related projects was world class, and I feel so fortunate to have had her focus, profound thoughts, and careful guidance.

Thanks also to: Bella Guzmán with Highwire Creative for the book cover and for the interior design and layout; Amy Hufford with Stellar Communications for designing the book's website presence; Janica Smith for managing the many administrative details that go into producing a book; and Dennis Welch for believing in me and being my biggest champion and publicist. I feel so blessed to have friends, colleagues and clients who have supported my journey and encouraged me to pursue this project. I especially want to thank my "peer review" group for taking the time and energy to give me feedback and ensure my content is interpreted as intended.

And finally, I am deeply grateful to my husband and family for their love, support and belief in me. They are my inspiration and help make it possible for me to do the work I love.

Leadership lives in the high visibility of center stage. We all know certain leaders who crave the spotlight, while others accept it reluctantly. Either way, their success positions them at the front of the corporate theater. Some leaders, however, take a different approach to that starring role. Rather than limiting their contact to the first few rows of the audience, they deliberately make the shift to leadership "in the round" for better access to the full spectrum of their operations.

Among the successful leaders who follow that philosophy is Frances Hesselbein, former CEO for *Girl Scouts of the USA* and current executive director with the *Leader to Leader Foundation*. Hesselbein likes to run her organizations from the center, using something she calls "circular management." We can learn two important lessons from this idea of 360° leadership and the people like Hesselbein who have used it successfully.

First, leaders who purposely increase their visibility throughout more layers of the corporate hierarchy can gain a number of advantages. For example, the CEO of a small publishing firm I know makes a habit of frequenting the shipping room when book orders are heavy. Rolling up his sleeves to pack boxes sends a powerful message to his team that everyone shares the workload, and the experience allows him to gather direct feedback from a more diverse group of employees. That increased sense of awareness gives him the insight to make better business decisions when he returns to the executive suite.

The second lesson we can take away from this concept is the understanding that visibility is a two-way street. Putting ourselves in a position on the leadership stage *to see* more clearly also allows us *to be seen* more clearly. In times of crisis, a highly visible leader can reassure employees that someone is in command and everything will be okay. However, the intense scrutiny isn't just reserved for those moments. Giving others a 360° view of everything we say and do comes with some risk.

Since the people around us have the vantage point to see things we sometimes can't, they often view our behaviors and communications in a very different light. They may or may not know our true intent, and that can occasionally lead to negative interpretations. Unless leaders (or those seeking to advance) are actively looking for those potential misperceptions and working to correct them, their leadership presence can be undermined, their reputations can erode, and even the most promising careers can be derailed. Sara Canaday refers to these unintentional misperceptions as our professional blind spots.

In her book, Sara connects the dots between perceptions, reputations and career success in a fresh, dynamic way. She uses insight and candor to help us identify our own blind spots, as well as providing specific ways to avoid and eliminate these insidious hazards. Through the detailed examples from her own coaching experience, she gives focus and clarity to a phenomenon that impacts everyone in the workplace but rarely gets discussed. For leaders (current and future) who want to accelerate their careers, Sara's book is the next best thing to having your own career coach.

Whether you are already standing in the leadership spotlight or working your way toward a starring role, think about your own leadership style. What do you want to project from center stage? More importantly, what does that look like to the people around you? How can you ensure that the performance your audience members experience is the same one you intended to give? *You – According to Them* can help professionals at any level discover how to consistently earn positive reviews.

John Baldoni is the president of Baldoni Consulting LLC, a full-service executive coaching and leadership development firm. John is a regular contributor to leading business websites such as HBR.com and Inc.com. John is internationally recognized as a thought leader and is the author of many books on leadership that have been translated into multiple languages through Europe and Asia. Recent titles include "Lead Your Boss," "Lead By Example" and "Lead With Purpose: Giving Your Organization a Reason to Believe in Itself." Readers are welcome to visit his website at www.johnbaldoni.com.

TABLE OF CONTENTS

PERCEPTION GAP:
Highly productive and innovative?
Or rebellious and uncooperative?

PERCEPTION GAP:
Intelligent and well-qualified?
Or condescending and elitist?

PERCEPTION GAP:
Too Direct: Decisive and candid?
Or abrupt and insensitive?

Not Direct Enough: Supportive and personable?
Or soft and lenient?

PERCEPTION GAP:
Extremely energetic and driven?
Or relentless and unrealistic?

PERCEPTION GAP:
Composed and steady?
Or robotic and indifferent?

INTRODUCTION

"Reputation" is not a line item we can find on a corporate income statement. But honestly, it should be. Instead it's lurking in there, living pervasively below the surface of the carefully calculated revenues and expenses. And yet, the accountants can't assign a specific number to it. *Think about that for a moment.* Companies can leverage the incalculable perceptions of a great reputation into bottom-line success and a very real corporate advantage. Sadly, there's also the flip side. Companies can totally crash and burn because of negative reputations, despite solid product offerings. Perceptions may be unquantifiable, but they are infinitely powerful.

This book is designed to show you that the same principle applies to each of us as individuals. Once we understand the power of our personal reputations, we can begin to see how others' perceptions of us can impact *our* ability to compete in the marketplace—for jobs, for raises, for promotions. In the same way this concept works for the business world, we can accelerate our own journeys toward success by evaluating our reputations and taking action to elevate them. When we are perceived as we intend, the results eventually show up in our own version of the bottom line, whether that means higher salaries and bonuses or new leadership positions and opportunities. Taking control of the impact we have on others allows us to take control of our own careers. Strange as it might seem at first, perception analysis holds the key to enhancing our "personal market value" and improving our own income statements.

Perceptions may be unquantifiable,
but they are infinitely powerful.

At this point, your inner accountant may be objecting loudly to the idea of a non-quantitative game plan for career advancement. *"Analyzing reputations and exploring perceptions? I can't measure that! If you want to get ahead, earn an advanced degree or complete a professional certification. You need something concrete to differentiate yourself."* Unfortunately, an extra diploma may not be the best answer, or at least not the only one. That traditional line of thinking simply doesn't hold up in our current environment of corporate downsizing, cost-cutting and resource-slashing. Add in the dizzying pace of business made possible by mind-boggling advances in technology, and you can see why employees at all levels are up against the most intense competitive pressure ever. The fierce battle for job security demands fresh strategies and innovative weapons. The truth is, those who are most successful today at climbing the proverbial corporate ladder and leading with real impact gain their distinct edge from an *intangible* skill set. They know their own reputations, their strengths and weaknesses. They are outstanding communicators and listeners. And they have a clear understanding of how their words and actions are perceived by others. In a nutshell, they are simply more effective at *relating to other people* while applying their technical and business skills in all types of situations. These employees show up to the workplace armed with a different set of credentials that has proven to be far more powerful than an Ivy League diploma.

Some people might define these intangible skills as emotional intelligence or self-awareness. Wander the aisles of any Barnes & Noble, and you're likely to find dozens of books on these topics. Scientists and executives seem to agree that self-awareness is, in fact, a critical component for success in virtually any environment—our workplaces, our communities and even our families. This concept is perhaps most relevant in the business context, where success is quantifiable and typically measured in dollars and cents. If we want to advance professionally, we simply must understand our reputations, our impact on others, and the way we are perceived by our colleagues, co-workers and clients. And yet this angle is so often overlooked.

If this approach is so successful, why don't more people make an effort to increase their self-awareness? The reasons are pretty diverse. Some may think emotional intelligence sounds far too ethereal, while others might feel uncomfortable with the honesty involved in self-reflection. Working with leadership consultants and executive coaches can be an excellent way to develop these relational abilities, but few people can invest the time and money for individual guidance through the process.

Great reasons aside, those who want to compete effectively in the workplace (whether that means ensuring basic job security or fueling bold career moves) must take the initiative to learn these intangible skills and monitor their reputations, one way or another. In today's business world, it's no longer an option. Professional development is a necessity, and the responsibility for moving forward (or falling behind) lies with each individual. That's precisely why I wrote this book.

If we want to advance professionally, we simply must understand our reputations, our impact on others, and the way we are perceived by our colleagues, co-workers and clients.

Before we dive in, let's explore a few of the key concepts used throughout the chapters ahead.

The Impact of Perceptions

As I already mentioned, volumes of pages have been written about the topics of self-awareness and the so-called "soft skills" that are critically important for leadership and communicating a professional presence. But here's what you need to know: virtually every aspect involved with improving our self-awareness comes down to *perceptions*. Understanding them. Changing them. Managing them. And perceptions actually hold the key to our reputations, personally and professionally.

So how much do you really know about perceptions today? Think about the story line from your favorite courtroom drama. The attorneys on both sides work feverishly to identify eyewitnesses with accounts of the crime du jour that support their legal strategy. Besides viewing the event from a physically different vantage point, all of the witnesses have a "personal filter" that affects what they notice and how they interpret the incident in question. For instance, an auto mechanic might be able to identify the exact make and model of a vehicle leaving a crime scene. A fashion editor might only have noticed the car's color, but could recall unique features of the suspect's clothing. Literally and figuratively, they see something different while witnessing the same event. Neither perception is wrong. *Just different.*

Now make the shift from the courtroom to the boardroom. The same concept applies to meetings, presentations and one-on-one conversations. Each person leaves the scene of an interaction with a different perception of what happened. That's normal. But if you find that your communication with others is frequently misinterpreted, received negatively or simply not as effective as it could be, inaccurate perceptions could be the culprit. And your reputation might be at risk.

The Dangers of Perception Gaps

To determine if perception gaps or disconnects could be derailing your career progress, take a moment and ask yourself some tough questions. When you interact with others, are you really sending the messages you intend? For instance, do your colleagues think of you as assertive? Or overbearing? Collaborative or manipulative? Gregarious or obnoxious? There's a fine line between these perceptions, but you can see why the subtle differences could have a huge impact on your career and your future.

When it comes to interpreting the impact of our communication with others, we all have blind spots that need our attention.

Perhaps the more important questions come next: how are you contributing to the perception gap? What are you doing in your interactions with others that prevents you from being more successful? What obstacles do you need to overcome to better manage the perceptions held by the people around you? By analyzing those perceptions—*your reputation, as defined by your co-workers*—you can identify the disconnects and strategically change your behavior to correct them, establishing a serious competitive advantage in your journey toward success.

It's definitely worth noting that misperceptions are an equal-opportunity interpersonal hazard: *no one is exempt from the effects of this phenomenon, including me.* When it comes to interpreting the impact of our communication with others, we *all* have blind spots that need our attention. They are subtle and hard to detect. On the other hand, you'll be happy to know there is a silver lining to that undeniable truth. Illuminating our blind spots isn't exclusively about uncovering negative behaviors. This process can also help us identify areas of untapped potential—our personal strengths that others see clearly but we haven't yet recognized or nurtured. *(See Figure 1 on Page 10 for more details.)* Either way, what we don't know *can* hurt us. And it often does.

The Power of Applied Self-Awareness™

Simply knowing that a problem exists doesn't fix it. Likewise, becoming aware of our reputations is only useful if we do something to make improvements. While the term "self-awareness" seems to imply a passive state of knowledge, I prefer to focus on the process of **applied self-awareness™**—*an active, ongoing brand of perception management that is truly the heart and soul of a stellar reputation.* You have to change your behavior to change the end result for yourself, as well as helping to drive better results for the people around you.

Essentially, applied self-awareness moves us from *insight* to *action.* In its very simplest form, successfully managing our reputations involves a strategic approach with two basic steps.

1	**SELF-AWARENESS** Identifying the gaps between how our words and actions are perceived versus how we intended them
2	**APPLIED SELF-AWARENESS** Using that information to adjust our behavior and close the gaps

When we can deliberately change our behavior in a way that allows our words and actions to be perceived precisely as we intended them, we can achieve the reputation and the results that we want.

By analyzing perceptions—*your reputation, as defined by your co-workers*—you can identify the disconnects and strategically change your behavior to correct them, establishing a serious competitive advantage in your journey toward success.

Getting Started

Uncovering and repairing our own perception gaps can generate a surprisingly wide range of career benefits. That's exactly why so many of my extended corporate workshops and in-depth coaching sessions center on this very topic. For those of you who are ready to tackle the process on your own, this book is designed to guide you through using an efficient, just-tell-me-the-bottom-line approach. Think of it as a do-it-yourself coaching tool. If you recognize the value of managing your professional reputation, this book is the effective short-cut you need: *refreshingly "light" on psychobabble, "heavy" on real-world applications, and laser-focused on getting results through action.*

In the chapters that follow, I describe the specific struggles of actual professionals—smart, hard-working people just like you—who initially couldn't see the perception gaps that were undermining their reputations and sabotaging their success. Pulled directly from my own coaching experience, each case study details one of these blind spots and examines the damage left in its wake. Chances are, you may see yourself (or possibly some of your co-workers) in these examples and be able to pinpoint which blind spots could be preventing you from reaching your full potential. Remember, I've also faced some of these challenges in my own career, so try to push past the denial when a scenario begins to sound uncomfortably familiar.

If the blind spot described in the first part of a particular chapter resonates with you, the second portion of that chapter offers valuable support to help you make a positive impact on your professional reputation. The *Perception 9-1-1* pages will give you "five fast fixes" you can use immediately to begin closing your perception gap. The Applied Self-Awareness charts at the end of the chapter provide a more comprehensive action plan you can follow for a long-term solution. I encourage you to customize these recommendations to help meet your own goals, and I've provided some space below each item to jot down your personal thoughts and ideas. I think you'll discover that each chapter includes concise, relevant guidance to help you close your personal perception gaps, repair reputation snafus, and make targeted changes with the real potential to boost your personal market value. Trust me, your inner accountant will be pleasantly surprised.

"Oh, what a great gift we would have if we could only see ourselves as others see us."

ROBERT BURNS
(Scottish Poet)

FIGURE 1

Do You See What I See?

A visual representation of perception gaps, the Johari Window is a well-known model for self-awareness and personal development. It can also be used to help us think about the barriers we face in our communications with the people around us. The model's four quadrants give us a framework to understand the concept that our colleagues' perceptions of us are not always identical to the perceptions we have of ourselves.

The Johari Window

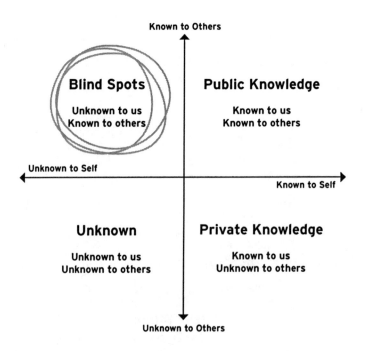

YOU — ACCORDING TO THEM   10

What Does It Mean?

The Upper Right Quadrant (*public knowledge*) includes the traits and information known by us and by others.

The Upper Left Quadrant (*blind spots*) is the unfortunate home of perception disconnects. Our colleagues recognize things about us in our interactions that we simply don't see, and that leads to a precarious perception gap. This is the place where confusion and misunderstanding can undermine our best efforts *or* where our most valuable talents and gifts are waiting silently to be unwrapped.

The Lower Right Quadrant (*private knowledge*) features communications that do not involve sharing fully with our colleagues, for better or worse. In some cases, it is perfectly appropriate to keep certain information private.

The Lower Left Quadrant (*unknown*) represents the unknown for us, as well as those around us. Communications in this quadrant can be shifted to the upper left quadrant (through observation and feedback from our colleagues, transforming them into blind spots) or shifted to the lower right quadrant (through self-discovery of attributes yet to be disclosed to others).

This book focuses on the career-stalling blind spots that occur in the upper left quadrant of the Johari Window. Using these chapters as your guide, you can take the steps necessary to move more of your behavior and communications into the upper right quadrant, ultimately closing the perception gaps that are preventing you from reaching your full potential.

CHAPTER 2

Don't Fence Me In

Clint was a 35-year-old sales professional with a captivating smile and a firm handshake. His enthusiasm made a lasting impression on the people he met, and his communication skills were quite strong. Also to his credit, Clint had a memory like a steel trap. Months or even years later, he could remember faces, names and facts with remarkable detail—a valuable asset in the world of sales. Combining that ability with his natural charisma, he had a real talent for snagging great job offers wherever he interviewed. His resume featured an impressive parade of Fortune 1000 firms as previous employers. However, the unusually long length of that parade hinted at a serious problem.

Clint struggled to remain employed with any company for more than a year. In fact, he spent the better part of his career changing jobs, industries and even states. At first glance, that nomadic employment behavior seemed odd for someone with such obvious skills and a proven history of sales success. He consistently met or exceeded his assigned sales goals, and he usually developed great rapport with his co-workers and staff members. So why did all of these blue-chip companies hand Clint a pink slip if he didn't run for the door first?

Buoyed by his ample self-confidence, Clint seemed to believe the value he brought to each employer gave him permission to bypass the companies' written *and* unwritten rules. He didn't feel the need to follow the Purchasing department's procedures for turning in expense reports. He skipped the company picnic because that would infringe on his personal time. And, despite the standard for business-casual attire, he sometimes showed up at the office wearing shorts. He was the employee who would sit down to craft a detailed memo to the CEO pointing out the flaws in the latest company policy. According to Clint, it was his job to shake things up. Even his *duty*. And seriously, what difference would it really make if he didn't attend the team's off-site social gathering? As long as he was exceeding his sales goals, everything else should be irrelevant. Needless to say, Clint felt very comfortable with his color-outside-the-lines approach.

Clint's managers initially agreed. They tried to cut him some slack because of his exceptional performance. At least for the first few months. Although his sales figures did produce the "wow factor," his supervisors soon grew weary of his "rules don't really apply to me" stance. While every other employee considered corporate procedures and events to be mandatory,

Clint viewed them as optional. He felt and acted like an exception to every rule.

That attitude became an uphill battle for which Clint's managers quickly lost the enthusiasm to fight. Whatever benefits he brought to the company were just not worth the trouble of trying to get him on board with policies or directions handed down from senior management. And before long, Clint was busy sending out more resumes once again.

While every other employee considered corporate procedures and events to be mandatory, Clint viewed them as optional. He felt and acted like an exception to every rule.

Perception Disconnect

Clint suffers from what I refer to as *Don't Fence Me In* syndrome. This professional blind spot affects those who are often quite successful but habitually resist what they perceive to be the cruel constraints of authority—unnecessary rules that limit their individuality, their creativity and, most of all, their freedom. These are the people who perform well but hit a major roadblock when it comes to following the standard procedures. If they are "ordered" to do something, they instantly feel emotionally claustrophobic.

If Clint were a cowboy, he'd essentially be saying: *"I'm happy to compete in your rodeo, and I'll probably win. But you need to find some new judges, because the current ones are incompetent.*

And your arena is way too small, so I'll be participating in the big open pasture two miles down the road." No thanks, cowboy. This rodeo will be just fine without you.

Those who are plagued by *Don't Fence Me In* syndrome seem to struggle with the fact that business is a game. Assuming they want to be employed and earn a paycheck, they've chosen to play the game. So—like it or not—they need to follow the basic rules. Certainly, no one is suggesting that companies would be better off with an army of cookie-cutter, order-following Stepford wives for employees. Creative thinking is critical for companies to gain a competitive edge and differentiate their products and services in unique ways. On the flip side, every business has certain "rules of engagement" that define its corporate culture and provide a proven structure to support the next great innovation. You can't play Monopoly if someone throws out the board.

This professional blind spot affects those who are often quite successful but habitually resist what they perceive to be the cruel constraints of authority.

Corporate renegades like Clint are typically quick to identify the *external* factors that have plagued their careers, from lousy supervisors to preposterous corporate strategies. From Clint's perspective, he would rather move on than be forced to work within the parameters of such narrow-minded leadership. Clint believed that taking a stand against corporate policies and customs demonstrated his leadership and ingenuity, but his managers simply perceived him as difficult and defiant.

Highly productive and innovative?

PERCEPTION GAP

Or rebellious and uncooperative?

If you think you might have a tendency toward *Don't Fence Me In* syndrome, give some thought to why you consciously (or subconsciously) resist authority and bristle at the idea of playing by the rules. Does this pattern reflect some lingering resentment from your past and perhaps an unfulfilled quest to express your independence? Were you permanently scarred by the personality style of a dominant or ineffective manager? Or—*prepare for a potentially awkward moment here*—does your ego simply get a bit carried away because of your superior performance? Exploring these possible causes may help you become more effective at managing your leader-resistant responses.

People who fall into the *Don't Fence Me In* category should begin to think about the structure and norms of business in a new way. Just because you follow those basic rules doesn't mean that you are being smothered by authority or shamelessly catering to office politics. Playing the game is a smart, savvy way to get ahead…not a humiliating, white-flag-waving surrender. Making that critical shift in thinking is one of the most important steps you can take to begin changing your reputation as a rebel among supervisors and managers.

> Just because you follow the basic rules doesn't mean that you are being smothered by authority or shamelessly catering to office politics.

It may also help to look at the game of business from a broader perspective. Together, you and your company are battling the competition. You're on the same side rather than being opponents. Will your actions or advice support your company's ability to succeed (and, coincidentally, its ability to pay your salary)? Or are you throwing a giant wrench into the well-oiled machine just to watch the sparks fly? While you are on the payroll, your success and your company's success are solidly intertwined. Remind yourself: *it's a teamwork thing*. And as the old saying goes, you don't want to cut off your nose to spite your face.

Unlike an exasperating teenager who argues for the sake of arguing, professionals with *Don't Fence Me In* syndrome may actually have noble intentions. They often believe they have a valid and even valuable purpose behind their conflicts with authority. They may even feel an obligation to share their viewpoints for the greater good of the organization. Without a doubt, successful companies need employees with innovative ideas and the confidence to share them. But in the midst of following these good intentions, the central issue with this blind spot emerges. People with *Don't Fence Me In* syndrome have trouble determining exactly *how* or *when* to provide their input gracefully.

Start by determining whether you should actually voice your objection in a particular situation. Will you be viewed as attacking a non-negotiable rule or process? Are you genuinely striving for innovation or simply asserting your dominance? Are you championing a fresh idea or just trying to get your own way? Can you make accommodations to support your team without sacrificing your beliefs or personal time?

If you decide to speak up, find out who should actually receive that input and investigate the optimal format and timing to share the information. Make sure that you provide your comments in a way that feels positive and supportive (rather than forceful and adversarial). While there are no specific guidelines for disagreeing with a cultural norm or tradition, you can develop a basic strategy for responding with more finesse.

People with *Don't Fence Me In* syndrome
have trouble determining exactly how or
when to provide their input gracefully.

The key is to recognize that fine line between providing helpful suggestions and creating unnecessary diversions from standard protocol. When a corporate team is distracted, performance and productivity take a huge nosedive. Keeping a tighter rein on your nonconformist tendencies may be one of the best ways to help your team generate better results. And should you decide to offer a dissenting opinion, pay very close attention to how you go about it.

PERCEPTION 9-1-1

Five Fast Fixes for
Don't Fence Me In Syndrome

1. **Reframe the picture.** Look at following the rules and taking orders in a different light. You aren't being *forced* to change; you are *choosing* to play the game with a different strategy—one that will ultimately be more successful.

2. **Go with the flow.** If you notice a pattern of objecting to anything and everything, step back. Do you really disagree with an idea or concept? Or is saying "no" a habit that helps you feel more in control of the situation and less restricted by the people in charge? If it's the latter, remind yourself to be flexible.

3. **Ignite your team spirit.** In the game of business, you and your company are wearing the same jerseys. For the good of the team, focus on working together to achieve your goals rather than constantly fueling your flair for individuality.

4. **Study the stars.** Find the people in your company who are playing the game well—adhering to the cultural norms yet still differentiating themselves as high-potential leaders. In what situations do they speak up to challenge an assumption? And how do they do it? Watch closely and take notes.

5. **Tiptoe through the minefield.** When you do feel the need to disagree, tread lightly. Express your opinions to the right person at the right time. Thoughtfully select your words and tone. Position your objections in a way that demonstrates your concern for the company's best interests.

Clint's Call for Help

After Clint parted ways with yet another employer, his frustration level reached new heights. One of our mutual friends gave him my name and suggested he contact me for an objective look at his bumpy career path. As we sat down at the conference table for our first meeting, he cut right to the chase with one simple question: *"Why does this keep happening to me, over and over again?"*

I asked Clint to describe what led up to his departure from the last few companies. His response included a stream of vivid details about power-hungry supervisors, clueless management teams and inane corporate policies. He seemed particularly annoyed with the occasional requests to participate in after-hours events that infringed on his own free time. There was an obvious theme running through Clint's tumultuous career: his defensive posture toward taking directions from his superiors and adapting to company rituals. He had a classic case of *Don't Fence Me In* syndrome.

Clint was so sensitive to being controlled that virtually every action and decision he made was colored by how he could avoid being managed. If he followed the rules, he felt like a disappointing suit sell-out.

When we discussed the possible reasons behind his hair-trigger resistance toward anything that threatened his autonomy, he immediately talked about his first job out of college. He explained that he worked for a man who had a real zest for climbing the corporate ladder. Clint viewed this man as inordinately demanding, as well as condescending. While many people feel taken for granted by their bosses at some point, this sounded like a constant drain on Clint's professional self-esteem. After 16 grueling months, he walked out and vowed never again to be controlled or abused by another employer.

Following that experience, Clint seemed to push back against anything and everything that even remotely seemed like a demand from upper management. To give in would be a sign of weakness and submission. Apparently that reaction became an automatic response for Clint. No matter where he worked, he couldn't seem to view a manager as a helpful guide and supporter. He only saw a threatening antagonist charged with keeping every employee confined to the company's prescribed "personality cubicle." He was so sensitive to being controlled that virtually every action and decision he made was colored by how he could avoid being managed. If Clint followed the rules, he felt like a disappointing suit sell-out.

With Clint's long history in sales, I wanted to show him the parallel between being a successful salesperson and being a successful employee. I first asked Clint to tell me about the techniques he used to generate new business and make a sale with a prospective client. He was quite animated in his description of the process: learning to "speak their language," demonstrating an understanding of their needs, gaining credibility, developing trust, and showing a sincere interest in helping them succeed long-term. He clearly understood that a good salesperson is very much like a chameleon, blending in and creating a sense of sameness that puts others at ease. My response was direct: if you are willing to mirror the values of a client's business to make the sale, wouldn't the same principle apply to your own company?

When Clint thought about it that way, he instinctively understood the idea. By respecting the culture, norms and traditions of his employer, he could build credibility and trust in a way that would enhance his career.

In one of our subsequent meetings, Clint and I talked about the difference between following the basic rules and losing all semblance of his individuality. I pointed out that the strongest branches on the tree are the ones that can bend without breaking in the fierce winds. The branches that refuse to bend are the ones that snap off quickly and get tossed to the ground. Being flexible and adapting to cultural norms are signs of strength and business savvy, not helplessness. We used some role-playing exercises to help him learn to identify when it was appropriate to push back against a cultural norm in a respectful way versus adapting to improve the end result for the corporate team. This was a new mindset for Clint, but I could tell he was beginning to make the shift.

By respecting the culture, norms and traditions
of his employer, Clint could build credibility and
trust in a way that would enhance his career.

Shortly after that, Clint landed a new job and reported that he was applying the thought processes we discussed with positive results. He was using his external sales techniques on his internal clients. He was paying close attention to the strategies used by the company's top executives who worked within the accepted cultural norms yet successfully set themselves apart.

He seemed to be embracing the concept that his talents and skills could be fully utilized within the confines of the corporate structure and existing rules.

The last time I spoke with Clint, he told me that he had remained employed with that company for several years—the longest tenure of his entire career. He added that he was now starting his own business, and he was excited about the opportunity to establish the norms and policies that would define his new workplace. I felt certain that the same increased self-awareness that enabled Clint to be better managed would serve him well in his capacity as a manager and owner.

"Individual commitment to a group effort—that is what makes a team work, a company work, a society work, a civilization work."

VINCE LOMBARDI
(Legendary U.S. Football Coach)

APPLIED SELF-AWARENESS

If your professional blind spot might be *Don't Fence Me In* syndrome, these action items will guide you through the process of making some positive changes:

1 Look for the root of the problem. Why does following the rules make you feel emotionally claustrophobic? Have you always balked at authority? Or when did that pattern begin? Understanding the cause of this blind spot will give you greater control over your inner rebel.

My Action Items: _____

_____

_____

_____

2 Remember that business is a game. Adopt the mindset that you have chosen to play the game. Following the rules is a proactive strategy to help you win, not behavior being forced upon you at gunpoint.

My Action Items: _____

_____

_____

_____

_____

3 Find role models within the company who can successfully present unconventional ideas while working within the framework of the corporate culture. Follow their lead. If you are still struggling to identify the unwritten rules of the workplace, ask straight out.

My Action Items: _____

_____

_____

4 Develop a specific strategy for presenting different approaches in the most influential and effective ways. Use a cooperative tone rather than an adversarial one. Choose words that demonstrate your posture as a team player rather than a solo act. And make sure you share your thoughts with the right person at the appropriate time.

My Action Items: _____

_____

_____

5 Practice mentally working through authority-driven scenarios with productive results. Before responding to actual situations, think about those successful behaviors and communication patterns. Breathe. Count to ten. Whatever it takes to suppress your authority-averse reaction and substitute a more effective one.

My Action Items: _____

_____

_____

6 Challenge yourself to see things from your boss' perspective or the company's viewpoint. Consider the reasons behind the rules or regulations in place, and try to give the benefit of the doubt. Resist the urge to assume that someone is trying to take advantage of you or doesn't trust your judgment.

My Action Items: _____

_____

_____

_____

_____

7 Present a positive attitude (rather than a sense of irritation) when you attend after-hours events such as social gatherings or team-building exercises. View them as an opportunity, instead of an imposition. Be ready to engage with your colleagues, and genuinely focus on developing stronger relationships. The connections you nurture in a more casual setting might just be the catalyst for getting to lead the big project or receiving your next promotion.

My Action Items: _____

_____

_____

_____

_____

8 Work on your impulse control. Identify the physical signs that you are feeling stifled by authority. Does your blood pressure go up? Does your face turn red? Does your breathing become more labored? If you sense the stress level is climbing, take extra caution to shut down the external responses that broadcast your discomfort (eye rolling, clinched jaws, exasperated sighs, closed body language).

My Action Items: _____

_____

_____

9 Enlist the support of a trusted colleague to offer real-time feedback. Ask this person to provide a subtle signal if you appear to be launching into an unnecessary, authority-focused attack.

My Action Items: _____

_____

_____

10 Consider a position or career that allows you to break away from a hierarchical structure and be your own boss. If you simply can't break the habit of championing unsanctioned approaches, you might find success and happiness as a trailblazing entrepreneur.

My Action Items: _____

_____

_____

CHAPTER 3

Intellectual Snob

Trish worked as a career advisor for one of the nation's top business schools. She landed this coveted position thanks, in part, to her impressive resume. Trish had earned an MBA with high honors from Stanford University and was selected from thousands of applicants for a unique international internship. No doubt about it, she was one smart cookie.

Trish also had a genuine talent for helping soon-to-be graduates pinpoint the career paths that best match their aptitudes and personalities. Her insightful recommendations frequently guided students toward previously overlooked areas that allowed them to embark on promising careers and, ultimately, reach their full potential. In sharp contrast, Trish's own career seemed to be hopelessly stalled.

When opportunities came up for an advisor to travel to other schools as a representative of the university, Trish's colleagues inevitably got the nod. If a leadership position was available, Trish's name never made the short list of candidates. Instead, she was usually tapped to head up quantitative analysis projects or to create trend reports for her unit. The pattern became obvious, and her frustration became overwhelming. She was haunted by the irony: *"if I'm so good at helping others reach their potential, why can't I seem to reach mine?"*

Trish's co-workers *could* have answered that question but, of course, they didn't. While she was understandably proud of her academic achievements and high IQ, Trish subconsciously developed a sense of intellectual entitlement. Whether intentional or not, her behavior suggested that she didn't see any value in working with colleagues or supervisors who hadn't graduated from a top-ten business school. For Trish, it was all about the pedigree; no mutts allowed. Somewhere along the line, her pride had morphed into pretentiousness. Perhaps she wasn't even aware of the change, but her borderline-boastful posture seeped into every conversation and left those around her feeling inferior and incompetent.

Perception Disconnect

Despite Trish's mental prowess and impressive credentials, the superior undertone in her attitude was undermining her success. Trish was an *Intellectual Snob.*

People with *Intellectual Snob* syndrome are the managers or colleagues who subconsciously communicate feelings of self-importance based on their impressive academic achievements or IQs. Sometimes their messages and tone can be subtle. Other times, not so much. Are they unusually smart? Yes! Do they have resumes to die for? Certainly! But those rock-solid competitive advantages are quickly washed away by their sometimes snooty demeanor—even if it is unintentional.

People with *Intellectual Snob* syndrome subconsciously communicate feelings of self-importance based on their impressive academic achievements or IQs.

Colleagues without the high-caliber background may perceive that the *Intellectual Snob* is overly critical and not-so-patiently tolerating what is judged to be their less-than-adequate performance. When interacting with those they do classify as their mental peers, *Intellectual Snob*s tend to throw down the brainpower gauntlet as their naturally competitive spirit emerges. They roll out the big vocabulary words, ramp up the use of lofty concepts, and race ahead with communications that may seem almost-purposely convoluted. Some of their peers may feel too ashamed to admit they don't understand and end up contributing in an ineffective (or worse, counterproductive) manner. The ones who do ask for clarification receive a disdainful response that leaves them feeling confused and belittled. The reputation of the *Intellectual Snob* is constantly eroded by a cascade of negative perceptions.

Many times, *Intellectual Snob*s are completely unaware of the tone they are projecting. They may perceive themselves as communicating with a well-deserved authority, but everyone else perceives it as presumptuous and condescending. It's not necessarily *what* they say; it's *how* they say it. The difference can be very subtle, and that's exactly why *Intellectual Snob* syndrome is an important professional blind spot to identify and correct.

Intelligent and well-qualified?

PERCEPTION GAP

Or condescending and elitist?

To determine if you might be caught in a pattern of intellectual snobbery, think about the answers to these questions. Do you have a high IQ or a big-time resume? Does that make you secretly feel smarter than the people around you? Do you feel annoyed when others are unable to grasp your ideas or directions? Do co-workers seem frustrated after interactions with you? Do you frequently mention or refer to your credentials?

Analyze some recent conversations with colleagues, and ask yourself honestly if your attitudes and beliefs could have "polluted" your message. Look beyond what you actually said, and think about whether your tone or nonverbal communications could have inadvertently layered a negative perception on top of an essentially neutral or even positive message. The key to correcting *Intellectual Snob* syndrome is often about changing your tone, and that starts with reframing your thoughts.

To help with that process, begin by imagining a football game. One team includes a number of leading NFL draft picks, several former Heisman Trophy winners, and last year's Super Bowl MVP. The other team includes…well, a roster of good guys that most fans wouldn't recognize. Here's the thing to remember: none of that is relevant once these strikingly different teams take the field to compete. What does matter is performance in this particular game, during the next 60 minutes of playing time. The officials don't award points to the more accomplished team because they got really close to the goal line. They don't overlook penalties committed by the better team because they usually play such a clean game. Both teams have an equal opportunity to win *today*. Yes, the elite team has players with greater talent and potential. But if they fail to work together effectively, lose their focus or make mistakes, the "win" could go to the less-qualified team. The final scoreboard will measure today's performance only. Everything before the kick-off is irrelevant.

The key to correcting *Intellectual Snob* syndrome is often about changing your tone, and that starts with reframing your thoughts.

If you think your professional blind spot might involve being an *Intellectual Snob*, this example has two important messages for you. First, no matter how great you are on paper, you run the risk of losing the game if you don't perform *right now*. Think about your performance in the present tense. Block out the "virtual brownie points" you feel you've earned through your resume or past awards, and concentrate only on the best strategy to accomplish your current goals today. Then work toward accepting the idea that delivering your best performance will require boosting your emotional intelligence to match your IQ. Specifically, to succeed today, you need to think less about the skill set you've already mastered and focus on learning the new ones that can help you move forward professionally.

Second, remember that having the advantage in talent and potential doesn't matter if you don't work well as part of a team. Re-think your concept of competition. You probably have a long personal history of success based on your ability to outperform the people around you—with higher SAT scores, better grades, fancier titles, more hours of overtime. However, your strong competitive instincts may actually become a liability as your career depends more on inspiring team success than establishing individual dominance. Confirming that you are smarter than everyone else won't help you reach your corporate goals. In fact, it will hurt.

To succeed today, think less about the
skill set you've already mastered and focus
on learning the new ones that can help
you move forward professionally.

This is a very different mindset for someone who suffers from *Intellectual Snob* syndrome: team competition trumps individual rivalry. As your career progresses, your *personal* success depends on whether you can tap into the unique skills and talents of your colleagues and integrate them in a way that maximizes results *for all of you as a team*. Whether you are positioned as a leader or a peer, working more effectively with your team members is the key to elevating your own personal market value.

As your career progresses, your *personal* success depends on whether you can tap into the unique skills and talents of your colleagues and integrate them in a way that maximizes results *for all of you as a team.*

Once you become aware of the detrimental attitudes holding you back and see the real benefits of change, you'll be able to better monitor your communications—verbal and nonverbal—to weed out any subtle (or less-than-subtle) elements that could be sending the wrong messages. The good news? If you can attack this challenge like all of the others that made your resume so outstanding, you'll find that changing your negative perceptions can happen faster than you think. By making these mental shifts, you'll be able to fight those underlying habits and approach teamwork in a new way that eliminates being perceived as an *Intellectual Snob*. Your suggestions will feel more collaborative, your tone will lose its sharp edge, and your reputation will begin to improve.

Five Fast Fixes for
Intellectual Snob Syndrome

1. **Apply your confidence with a paint brush, not a sledge hammer.** Soften your interactions with others so you aren't perceived as overly confident. Offer your recommendations and knowledge with a deliberate sense of humility.

2. **Upgrade to a stronger filter.** Just like Mom always told you: *think before you open your mouth.* If there's any way that your words could be perceived as bragging or condescending, don't say them. Consider alternatives.

3. **Call in the Tone Police.** Despite the best choice of words, your tone of voice can completely contradict your message. Same thing for body language. "Intellectual superiority" comes through loud and clear, so be sensitive to *how* you say things.

4. **Become a talent detective.** Look for the unique strengths, skills and talents in others that are necessary for your team to reach its goals. Find them. Acknowledge them. Nurture them.

5. **Take on the role of perpetual student.** Instead of focusing on how much you know, concentrate on what you can still learn. Recognizing that you are always a novice in some area will temper your attitude with a much-needed dash of humility.

Trish's Response

When Trish realized that her career wasn't advancing on her usual lightning-fast trajectory, she contacted me for assistance. It was clear to me that Trish showed all the signs of being an *Intellectual Snob*. In fact, I detected that she was a little hesitant about working with me in the first place. Though I had earned an MBA, it certainly wasn't from a highly prestigious school. Not top 10. Not even top 20. And I could tell she was throwing little challenges my way, just to see where I stood on the intellect scale.

By our second meeting, I gave Trish my honest thoughts on why she wasn't (and probably wouldn't be) achieving her success potential. I gently explained that her intellectual gift was getting in the way of sharing and showcasing the amazing things she had the capability to achieve. By limiting most of her communications to a narrow audience of those she considered to be her intellectual peers, she was limiting her own market share. Plus, her ineffective delivery was watering down the impact of her great ideas. Until she took the time and energy to meet the people around her at their own intellectual comfort level, she wasn't going to meet them anywhere. Her unapproachable demeanor and Ph.D.-dissertation-worthy communication would always make it difficult for co-workers to ask for clarification.

Fortunately, Trish's desire to improve and enhance her leadership skills enabled her to overcome *Intellectual Snob* syndrome in short order. I helped Trish to see that influence was sometimes more important than sheer accuracy. Being "right" as an individual can get in the way of being productive as a team. Trish and I talked about mentally leveling the playing field, focusing on current performance, and approaching each colleague as a valued contributor with a unique and necessary talent required for reaching the team's goals. For the first time, Trish truly realized that group success was an integral part of her personal success.

Trish began to make changes—in her words, her tone, her body language and her interactions with others. Before long, she was able to move from being perceived as a "cognitively challenging facts only" kind of person to someone relatable, friendly and even helpful. Trish's sphere of influence expanded, as did the number of individuals she could collaborate with, trust, encourage and, eventually, ask for support.

The results of her changes were dramatic. As her emotional intelligence improved to the level of her book-smarts, Trish saw positive benefits on many fronts. She felt accepted and valued as part of the career advising team. Instead of resentment, she felt respect from her peers. New opportunities started coming her way. And today, Trish has happily (and humbly) moved into a top leadership position in her department.

"We should take care not to make the intellect our God. It has, of course, powerful muscles, but no personality."

ALBERT EINSTEIN
(Nobel Prize-Winning Physicist)

APPLIED SELF-AWARENESS

If your professional blind spot might be *Intellectual Snob* syndrome, these action items could help you make some positive changes:

1 Be honest with yourself: do you have an underlying attitude of superiority based on your intelligence or academic achievements? Remind yourself regularly that *how you relate to others* is just as important, if not more so, than *how much you know.*

My Action Items: _____

_____

_____

_____

2 Think about meeting your performance goals in the present tense. What you've already accomplished is irrelevant; what matters now is how you perform today and how effectively you work with the people around you.

My Action Items: _____

_____

_____

_____

_____

3 Communicate with others on their level, while being careful not to "talk down" to them. Translate complex ideas using personal anecdotes or common metaphors to help you connect with people at all intellectual levels.

My Action Items: _____

_____

_____

4 Adopt a new approach to teamwork. Instead of trying to compete with your colleagues, deliberately search for the unique talents that each person can contribute to help the team reach its collective goals. Visualize the talents of others as the bridge you need to cross over for greater success in your own career.

My Action Items: _____

_____

_____

_____

5 Tone down your dominance in dealing with others. If you can temper your bold confidence and strong opinions with a little finesse, you'll be perceived as influential instead of overbearing.

My Action Items: _____

_____

_____

_____

6 Pay close attention to your word choice as you communicate with others so you don't inadvertently undermine your own efforts to build stronger relationships. Limit the use of phrases like "as you know" and "obviously."

My Action Items: _____

_____

_____

_____

7 Accept that your way isn't the only way, and listen actively to find the merit in your colleagues' ideas. Resist the urge to immediately devalue the opinions of those who don't share your qualifications.

My Action Items: _____

_____

_____

_____

8 Use your strong skills in self-discipline to embrace this new attitude. Just as you have worked hard to succeed at everything else, you have the capacity to increase your emotional intelligence and reach your full potential.

My Action Items: _____

_____

_____

_____

CHAPTER 4

Frozen Compass

Jason worked as the director of media and research for a large advertising agency. His straight-talking, über-efficient style was, in many ways, a perfect fit for that position. In fact, if Jason were a product, his slogan would have been: *"just bottom-line it."* He was extremely organized, intensely focused and highly productive—all characteristics that made him uniquely qualified to handle the brutal demands and crazy deadlines of the agency world.

Even when inundated by statistics, Jason seemed to have a remarkably clear vision of exactly what needed to be done and by whom. He was known for delegating tasks at a brisk pace with his authoritative tone, and his colleagues clearly respected his ability to get things done. When the big account was in jeopardy or the presentation unexpectedly got moved up by two days, they knew they could count on Jason. No one seemed to complain that he wasn't a small-talk kind of guy. He got results, and that often made him a hero.

After 11 years of success in the agency world, Jason decided to integrate his media expertise with his entrepreneurial spirit and open his own firm. During the ramp-up phase, Jason's candid approach was a definite asset. His direct demeanor was ideal when meeting with attorneys and bankers, pitching angel investors, and setting up the infrastructure for his new business. Things got a bit more complicated once he started hiring the office staff.

Jason's get-to-the-point posture, one that was so effective in a specialized department at the agency, wasn't translating well with his new hires. Communicating his expectations or providing feedback to his employees on a broader scale had not been successful, despite his best intentions. When he pointed out team members' errors or pushed them harder, he wasn't just trying to build his business; he genuinely wanted to help them learn and succeed. Somehow that message wasn't getting through. The impact was taking a toll on Jason's ability to scale his business. He couldn't focus on adding new clients because he was constantly replacing employees.

On the other end of the spectrum, Michael was an easy-going district manager for a company that manufactures telecommunications equipment. He was universally admired throughout the company, and his teams had a stellar reputation for beating their performance goals. Using his likability as an advantage, Michael found success by connecting with his staff members, making them feel valued, and motivating them to perform at optimal levels through a shared sense of accountability. He was always interested in hearing about Allen's upcoming wedding, Kristen's trip to Italy, and Bob's home remodeling project. Michael generated loyalty and positive results by building rapport with his staff members on a deeper level.

As the competitive landscape in telecommunications became more ferocious, Michael's company was forced to make big changes. Budgets were slashed, and a major restructuring initiative gave the organization chart an extreme makeover. When the dust settled, Michael ended up with a different vice president calling the shots and a challenging new set of requirements designed to help the company stay afloat. The message booming down from upper management was clear: *pick up the pace!* At first subtly and then much less so, Michael was told to kick his department into overdrive. The performance goals were higher. The deadlines were shorter. And he was charged with keeping all of those increased expectations top-of-mind among his staff.

Jason and Michael experienced success in their careers by tapping into their own natural manner of communicating and interacting with others. Now the approaches that served them well for years were holding them back.

While this more forceful approach came easily for his new boss and many of his peers, it went completely against Michael's natural demeanor. In the analogy about motivating the mule, he definitely preferred to use the carrot rather than the stick.

Perception Disconnect

Jason and Michael have each experienced success in their careers by tapping into their own natural manner of communicating and interacting with others. Although they both were skilled at reaching the destination known as "results," they took very different routes to get there. In Jason's case, he traveled directly toward his desired end-point, even if that involved speeding and taking some sharp corners. For Michael, his travel involved the relaxed pace of a more scenic route. The ride was quite different, but they were both rewarded early on in their careers for making these journeys with their own unique style. Unfortunately, change reared its ugly head, as it inevitably does. The approaches that had served them well for years were now holding them back. Despite their differences, Jason and Michael were struggling with the same professional blind spot known as *Frozen Compass* syndrome.

Unless Jason and Michael can learn to "read"
new situations and adapt their styles, the positive
perceptions that they worked for years to establish
would not continue under the new circumstances.

People with *Frozen Compass* syndrome get stuck in a rut using their natural style of interacting with others, whether that might be very direct or indirect. Neither approach is wrong; the problem lies with the inability to change in certain settings. When external rules and parameters shift but their behaviors stay the same, perceptions of their performance by those around them can begin to deteriorate. Unfortunately, they are so comfortable following the same path that has always worked for them that they don't recognize the roadblock.

Like many of the blind spots in this book, *Frozen Compass* can be difficult to detect, but essential to identify and correct. Jason would only continue to be successful if he learned to be a little less direct and started to think "relational" instead of "rational." Michael would have to do the reverse, getting to the point more quickly and being more specific about deliverables and deadlines. Unless Jason and Michael can learn to "read" the new situations and adapt their styles, the positive perceptions that they worked for years to establish would not continue under the new circumstances.

Too Direct:
Decisive and candid? Or abrupt and insensitive?

PERCEPTION GAP

Not Direct Enough:
Supportive and personable? Or soft and lenient?

If you suspect that *Frozen Compass* syndrome might be your professional blind spot, take some time to analyze your personal work style. Start by defining your usual manner of interacting with other people. Do you take the direct route or do you prefer a more indirect path? How has that natural tendency been successful for you in the past? Have you been rewarded for that behavior? What has changed in your work environment since that time—people, policies or situations? Does your typical level of candor now seem less effective than it has been in the past? Try to pinpoint some examples where that might be to blame for lower productivity or even criticism.

Once you've recognized this blind spot—*the need to adjust how direct you are with others in certain environments*—you're ahead of the game. Now you can focus on making the necessary adjustments to close the inadvertent perception gap. Yes, you will have to step out of your behavioral comfort zone to reach your destination, but the path you usually travel is no longer getting you where you want to go. It might help to think about swapping your trusty compass for a GPS that can show you multiple routes to reach your destination. There's more than one way to get there, and it's time for a slight detour.

People with *Frozen Compass* syndrome get stuck in a rut using their natural style of interacting with others.

One of the primary tools you can use to minimize *Frozen Compass* syndrome is awareness—being more aware of your own behaviors and those of the people around you. Sometimes collaborating with others will require a bit more finesse and handholding. At other times, the direct approach is not only preferred but mandatory. By paying attention and learning to recognize subtle cues that a particular situation calls for a different approach, you can respond more quickly. With a little practice, you'll even learn to become proactive about the shift.

I would like to add one word of caution about resolving

Frozen Compass syndrome. It isn't about abandoning your usual approach altogether. Minor changes really can make a significant impact. Go slowly, and use moderation in making your adjustments. You can still leverage your own natural strengths, but strategically give them a nudge in the direction that helps you achieve better results in your new business climate.

Once you've recognized this blind spot—*the need to adjust how direct you are with others in certain environments*—you're ahead of the game.

Too Direct

If you tend to fall on the high end of the "directionally challenged" scale, make a conscious effort to moderate your pace. That doesn't mean you should begin ignoring deadlines or start playing Sudoku at your desk all afternoon. Just find times when it's appropriate to hit pause. And when you do, use that time to develop connections and build stronger relationships with your team members. Find things you have in common other than your office address. Show an interest in their lives outside of work, and don't be afraid to share something from your own. It's a two-way street.

Challenge your belief that directness is always correlated with efficiency and productivity. For instance, you might discover that making an effort up front to get your co-workers on board with a proposal and communicate more details will pay off in surprising ways. It might feel at first like an unnecessary step, but that investment of time could create valuable momentum and allow your team to reach its goals even faster. Remember that your colleagues and staff members aren't simply a means to an end on the current project; they will likely play a key role in meeting future goals as well, so it's to your advantage to keep them in the loop.

Challenge your belief that directness is always correlated with efficiency and productivity.

Get into the habit of giving others the chance to share their information and opinions before you speak up. This will probably catch them off guard at first, especially if they are accustomed to hearing you deliver definitive orders that don't seem to come with an invitation for discussion. Even the first few times you ask for feedback, your co-workers may not be sure you really want it. Keep trying and find ways to demonstrate that you value their input, even if you don't always choose to apply it. Over time, your willingness to listen and seek alternative ideas will help to create a more positive environment. And in turn, your colleagues will probably be much more eager to help you achieve your goals.

Not Direct Enough

For those of you who might need to rev up your level on the directness meter, think about the belief system behind your more timid approach. Then try to change your assumption that being too direct is overly abrupt or might somehow undermine the team atmosphere. Not all direct communication is disruptive or ineffective. Remember that people actually value honest, straightforward messages, and give yourself permission to try that approach. With a little practice, you can blend in more urgency and directness to your communications while not completely abandoning the softer touch that comes more naturally to you.

Consider letting your co-workers know why you are making some adjustments to your style. If they understand the reasoning behind the change, they will be more open to the shift (especially if you can also describe how they will benefit as well). Transparency and open communications will pave the way for a successful transition.

Sprinkle in more assertive language, and avoid the temptation to apologize or back-peddle. You can communicate politely and pleasantly, even if you have to relay a non-negotiable policy or deadline. Sometimes a sense of humor can even help to add a soft edge to a pointed message. Relationships still trump results, but shoot for a healthy balance.

Sprinkle in more assertive language, and avoid the temptation to apologize or back-peddle.

Using the same rule that applies for all of the blind spot adjustments, start with small changes. Going overboard is sure to create confusion. Imagine your colleagues' reactions if you showed up to the next meeting with what seemed to be a completely different personality. They might think you've lost your mind. Make gradual adjustments, and monitor the reactions along the way.

PERCEPTION 9-1-1

Five Fast Fixes for
Frozen Compass Syndrome

1. **Shift your latitude.** Buy yourself some time to adjust your approach by increasing your impulse control. Stop before you react, consider the impact of your natural response, and consciously shift your actual message in the right direction.

2. **Share your new map.** Instead of leaving your co-workers confused by your shift, take a moment to explain the change. And you get bonus points for demonstrating how they can also benefit from the adjustment.

3. **Explore alternate paths.** Anticipate the situations you will encounter today, and think about different options for communicating in a way that's more or less direct than your usual approach. You'll feel more comfortable trying something new if you've thought in advance about the words and tone that are likely to be most effective.

4. **Watch for detour signs.** As you shift your interactions with others, pay close attention for signs that they are confused or upset. Stop and ask for directions if you seem lost, and don't wait until you are hopelessly off course. Watch, listen and be proactive about staying on track.

5. **Find a travel partner.** Enlist the support of a trusted colleague to give you more direct feedback as you work to change your behavior and communication patterns.

Adjusting the Routes

Jason and I originally met at a national conference for entrepreneurs. During a small breakout session, we were randomly paired together as part of an exercise to gather objective input on our current business strategies. Our assigned task was to discuss some of the obstacles that were standing in the way of moving our organizations to the next level. In addition to sharing our stories, we were asked to function as "on the spot" business coaches for our partners.

When Jason began to describe the challenges he had faced since opening his media company, I remember cringing inside because the scenario sounded so familiar. As it turned out, Jason and I had a lot in common—specifically, *Frozen Compass* syndrome. My natural tendency was also to leap straight to the bottom line and put efficiency far above everything else on the priority list. I could easily understand his blind spot because I had lived it! Over the years, I developed quite a few strategies to compensate for my super-direct approach, and I was happy to share my first-hand experiences.

My initial suggestion to Jason involved striking a better balance between the productive and the personal in his written communications. Since those don't occur face-to-face in real-time, he'd have the luxury of making changes and trying some different options. Before sending out emails or letters, Jason could deliberately make final edits with the intent to soften his message. We talked about the impact of word choices on the tone of written communications that arrive without the benefit of facial expressions or body language. I also asked him to consider leading off his messages with a personal question or comment before diving in to a professional request or demand. Including something more personal would "warm up" his communications and help him to begin building stronger connections with his employees.

From there, I knew Jason would be able to extend that strategy into the live interactions with his staff members. He could deliberately infuse some personal comments into his status meetings or phone conversations to help balance out his results-focused nature. In addition, we explored the idea that most people want and need to know the context of certain goals and requests. Even when Jason felt compelled to assign a task by "stripping away the fat" and getting right to the desired deliverables, he could benefit by taking a moment to share the big-picture perspective and the thought process driving the request. Not only would that help his staff develop more positive perceptions about Jason, he would probably get greater cooperation from his employees and start to create more of a team atmosphere. If they felt more valued, they would also be more likely to cut Jason some slack if his overly direct approach were to slip back in from time to time.

As the owner of the company, Jason felt that he had an obligation (and even a right) to provide feedback on his employees' performance. He was, after all, paying their salaries. I agreed, but also challenged Jason to try something a little different. In my experience, I got better results by first asking permission to provide feedback rather than just blurting out a criticism in the heat of the moment. Timing is everything. If I waited until the appropriate time and delivered my message with tact and sincerity, I was consistently amazed at the reaction and positive response. In fact, many times I've been thanked for providing candid observations in a compassionate way. Jason appeared to be up for that challenge and was excited about trying that different approach.

In the years since Jason and I first met, his company has experienced steady growth. He admits that the first year was tough—while he was still learning to step outside of his directness comfort zone—but he formed new habits that are still serving him well today. He said the most important thing is reminding himself regularly to pay close attention to his behaviors and the reactions of his staff members. Jason eventually hired a director whose communication style complemented his, and she brought an excellent balance to the leadership team. His company's turnover rate had dropped, and his profits were up.

My initial suggestion to Jason involved striking a better balance between the productive and the personal in his written communications.

As for Michael, he has been a family friend for many years. I have often admired his combination of sharp business savvy and sophisticated emotional intelligence. He was known for making smart decisions and always maintaining a consistent, steady demeanor. Whether he was facing the demands of a high-pressure project or juggling his busy family life, Michael seemed perennially calm and happy. Not to mention successful. That's why I was truly puzzled when we met for dinner one evening and he mentioned growing concerns about his frustrations at work.

Once Michael described his company's changing expectations and the pressures he was feeling to adjust his leadership style, I knew that *Frozen Compass* syndrome was the culprit. He had spent years building rapport and camaraderie with his staff, utilizing his natural laid-back style. Now senior management was telling him to march into meetings with arms swinging and emphatically demand compliance with new policies and steep performance goals. *"That's just not how I get things done,"* he kept saying. What they were asking Michael to do ran completely counter to his usual approach.

My first recommendation to Michael was to meet with his staff and honestly tell them the backstory. Because they knew him fairly well, they would be confused if he made changes with no explanation. Instead, he could describe the new goals and expectations, helping them prepare for a shift in his tone. That information would give them context to process the change. He could even reveal to them that he wasn't completely comfortable with this new style, but encourage them all to work together in meeting the challenges of the "new order." The act of sharing this information with his close-knit team would reinforce the loyalty he had cultivated for many years. By using transparency, he could remain true to himself while complying with the demands of his managers.

Once Michael had a chance to lay the groundwork with his staff, I suggested a few ways he could begin beefing up the direct nature of his communications. When he gave orders, he could leave less room for rebuttal. He shouldn't feel the need to rationalize every request or provide more information than necessary. He could strive to be more candid when a team member's performance wasn't up to par. Michael could also make some physical changes to give his leadership a more direct edge. For instance, he could use a slightly louder voice and try to physically command more space in the room.

Michael started making small adjustments to his behavior and communications, and he was relieved to find that his team members seemed enthusiastic about supporting him during the changes. Over time, he found that he could ramp up his direct approach even more when needed and maintain the positive goodwill among his staff. He actually had more latitude than he ever imagined.

Michael's efforts were clearly successful. When the continued economic downturn caused his company to lay off more than half of its managers, Michael was grateful to be among those who kept their jobs. Then, as the company began to experience a new surge in growth, he was asked to take on exciting new responsibilities.

"Notice that the stiffest tree is most easily cracked, while the bamboo or willow survives by bending with the wind."

BRUCE LEE
(Chinese Martial Arts Expert & Actor)

APPLIED SELF-AWARENESS

If your professional blind spot might be *Frozen Compass* syndrome, you may find these action items helpful:

Frozen Compass: Too Direct

1 Reset your belief that peak efficiency is only possible with a direct approach. There are multiple ways to maximize productivity, and your current style isn't allowing you to reach your full potential. Be open to the idea that there is another alternative.

My Action Items: _____

_____

_____

_____

2 Use the wisdom of hindsight to think of specific examples when your direct approach seemed to hold you back. How could you have handled those situations differently to produce better results? Use those ideas as a starting point for the future.

My Action Items: _____

_____

_____

_____

3 Slow down. Your natural pace may be perceived as frenetic. If you recognize that the tempo of meetings or conversations is escalating, consciously reduce the speed.

My Action Items: _____

_____

_____

_____

4 Practice your impulse control. Resist the urge to instantly advise, question or jump right to the main point. When it's appropriate, be the last one to contribute. Take a backseat on occasion, and try not to exert your influence too early.

My Action Items: _____

_____

_____

_____

5 Solicit feedback from your team members. Participating in the process makes people feel valued. Even if you don't follow every suggestion, you'll reap the rewards from building a stronger sense of teamwork.

My Action Items: _____

_____

_____

_____

6 Actively listen as your co-workers share ideas. Pay attention to the full spectrum of what they are saying—their overall concepts, intentions, words and nonverbal signals. Try not to let your brain leap ahead to objections or better ideas. You might uncover an angle you missed.

My Action Items: _____

_____

_____

7 Move out of your comfort zone and try a new approach. Take steps to soften the direct nature of your written communications and personal interactions, and be sure to monitor the responses from your co-workers. Maintaining awareness will help you make continuous improvements.

My Action Items: _____

_____

_____

8 Adjust your style with gradual changes. A radical departure from your usual approach would be disconcerting. As with all of the blind spots, think of fine-tuning and balancing rather than jarring modifications.

My Action Items: _____

_____

_____

_____

Frozen Compass: Not Direct Enough

1 Test your assumptions. Just because communication is direct doesn't mean it is rude or ineffective. When it is used strategically, a direct approach can be seen as a sign of great leadership and can generate a wealth of positive perceptions.

My Action Items: _____

_____

_____

_____

_____

2 Think about recent interactions with managers and colleagues when your indirect approach might have given others a negative perception. Were there signals that could have helped you adjust your style? How can you use those experiences to adjust your behavior in the future? Be willing to try something new.

My Action Items: _____

_____

_____

_____

_____

3 Give context to your behavioral changes. When appropriate, share with your co-workers why you are making adjustments to your communication style. If they know the business conditions that are prompting the change, they are more likely to understand when you need to be less accommodating.

My Action Items: _____

_____

_____

4 Remember that most people value forthright, straightforward communication. Aim to provide feedback that is concrete and immediate. Rely on your ability to communicate direct messages in a fair, genuine and caring manner.

My Action Items: _____

_____

_____

5 Wear your authority with conviction. Whether we like it or not, communication clutter fights to drown out our messages; the loudest ones are more likely to be heard. Speak up, be decisive, and resist the tendency to apologize.

My Action Items: _____

_____

_____

6 Use physical cues to help your messages feel more direct. Take up more space in the room. Strive for a deeper voice, but raise the sound level a bit. Make sure that your facial expressions and tone support your words so that statements aren't interpreted as questions.

My Action Items: _____

_____

_____

_____

7 Leverage your strengths. If you have a long history of consistent and calm demeanor, that track record will balance your more assertive approach over the long-term.

My Action Items: _____

_____

_____

_____

8 Stay true to yourself as you shift your behavior to be more direct. Small changes can make a big difference, so don't feel the need to go overboard.

My Action Items: _____

_____

_____

CHAPTER 5

Dust in My Wind

Laura was an intelligent, gifted woman with an unparalleled work ethic and a penetrating drive to succeed. She possessed a photographic memory and the ability to remain highly focused and productive well beyond the limits of her peers. In fact, Laura had the level of stamina that would have qualified her as an Olympian if she weren't the CEO of a boutique health management company.

Right from the start, Laura's expertise in medical cost containment set her apart as a leader in her field. With each promotion and new job, she took on additional responsibility, a bigger staff and larger projects—ultimately moving into her current position at the helm of her own company. She loved the challenge of being an entrepreneur. And her clients loved the fact that she was incredibly dedicated to helping them succeed. Laura was adamant about providing her clients with exceptionally attentive service. (*"Need it today? No problem!"*) As she quickly built a reputation for helping companies to generate measurable business growth, her own client list continued to expand.

Laura's impressive, machine-like energy also earned her quite a reputation within the organization she had built: she was one of those bosses people loved to hate. Working with Laura meant gaining valuable business experience, learning innovative strategies and, of course, logging in obscene amounts of overtime to meet the challenging demands.

Laura's impressive, machine-like energy earned her quite a reputation within the organization she had built: she was one of those bosses people loved to hate.

While many people did excel under Laura's leadership, their business success often came at a heavy personal price. As these employees reached new heights of productivity under her tutelage, their worlds outside the realm of the office sometimes dropped to disappointing lows. Did they attribute their corporate accomplishments and professional development to working with Laura? Definitely. But, at times, they also blamed her for their outright exhaustion.

That probably explains why the turnover rate at Laura's company fluctuated quite a bit. Some employees simply couldn't take the constant pressure. And those who remained on board often experienced bouts of poor self-confidence with the inevitable comparison to Laura's extensive capabilities and relentless drive.

Laura was running marathons. Scratch that; Laura was *winning* marathons. But she had never paused long enough to recognize that most people weren't capable of performing the same super-human feats of endurance. Laura had taken her own capacity and tolerances for granted, assuming that they were the norm, the baseline from which she should measure all others. Meanwhile, some on her staff lagged behind—struggling, exhausted and burned out.

Perception Disconnect

Laura was unable to see that she suffered from what I call *Dust in My Wind* syndrome. *Dust in My Wind* is perhaps one of the biggest hurdles to identify and overcome. Why? Because the unstoppable, energy-packed leaders who possess this emotional blind spot have often been highly rewarded for their tireless behavior throughout their careers. They have achieved success and likely attribute that directly to their adrenaline-overloaded approach. The problem is, these high-capacity leaders aren't aware that they have been successful *despite this behavior*, not because of it.

Laura had taken her own capacity and tolerances for granted, assuming that they were the norm, the baseline from which she should measure all others.

People with *Dust in My Wind* syndrome have the potential to be extraordinary leaders. What organization wouldn't love to employ someone with unrivaled expertise and irrepressible stamina, endlessly driven to meet the next challenging goal? Here's the hitch. That intrinsic value disintegrates when they aren't aware of their own off-the-charts capacity, leaving colleagues around them feeling inadequate and defensive, struggling to keep up with a seemingly impossible pace. Those suffering with this blind spot usually have the best of intentions, but the good motives get lost in translation. While they readily admit to being ambitious, they are completely oblivious to the surprising magnitude of their own capabilities—to effortlessly work longer hours, produce more, and get better results than the average person. Honestly, better than most people. Their colleagues have a vastly different perception.

Extremely energetic and driven?

PERCEPTION GAP

Or relentless and unrealistic?

Those who suffer from *Dust in My Wind* look at the requirements to achieve particular objectives according to *their* personal levels of performance, defining and measuring everything by their own uniquely high standards and abilities. They don't always understand that the people around them have different skill sets and approaches that may be equally valid and, sometimes, even more successful.

If you're wondering whether *Dust in My Wind* syndrome applies to you, start by looking for clues among those around you. Do the people who usually work hard to please you seem to be slowly running out of steam? Have you sometimes heard passive-aggressive comments disguised as humor in staff meetings? Have you noticed normally even-keeled people becoming highly emotional or competitive with their counterparts, doing anything they can to keep up? Identifying these signs may be the catalyst to help you adjust your expectations before you inadvertently push your team members to the breaking point.

Those who suffer from *Dust in my Wind* look at
the requirements to achieve particular objectives
according to their personal levels of performance,
defining and measuring everything by their
own uniquely high standards and abilities.

In the absence of observable signals, you may have to ask someone you trust for direct feedback. One point worth mentioning: it takes a very brave soul to bring this type of blind spot to the attention of a co-worker, especially if you happen to be the boss. Sometimes the point isn't made until an exit interview (theirs or yours). Of course, by then it may be too late to salvage an important working relationship or a position within a particular company.

Overcoming the *Dust in My Wind* syndrome requires slowing down, accurately measuring the true performance capacity of your colleagues, and adjusting your expectations to be more realistic. Not that you shouldn't strive for higher goals or better performance…just make sure your vision is framed in a practical, achievable context.

Moving forward, take the time to recognize the unique gifts and talents of each individual who participates on your team. Express appreciation for the contributions of others, and make a deliberate effort to give them credit *every chance you get.* When you're aware of your tendency to travel at top speed, you can remind yourself to take your foot off the gas pedal and, metaphorically speaking, acknowledge the other drivers.

Overcoming the *Dust in My Wind* syndrome requires slowing down, accurately measuring the true performance capacity of your colleagues, and adjusting your expectations to be more realistic.

Great leaders know how to reduce their pace to find the team's optimal rate of speed. They can strategically shift their focus outward—away from their own standards of performance—so they can evaluate the needs of their colleagues and, ultimately, create a team with the potential for greater results. In fact, leaders who have worked hard to correct *Dust in My Wind* through strategic behavior change are usually surprised at the wide range of unexpected benefits. They notice that staff members seem more relaxed and focused, less emotional and irritable. Relationships in the office become stronger. Teamwork improves, and morale makes a quantum leap forward. Best of all, the organization can still meet its goals and keep performance metrics high.

PERCEPTION 9-1-1

Five Fast Fixes for
Dust in My Wind Syndrome

1. **Pay attention to traffic.** Flying along in the fast lane might be standard procedure for you, but monitor the speed of the people around you. Successful teamwork requires being ready to "merge"—without running everyone else off the road.

2. **Show your human side.** Chances are, your co-workers may think of you as a results machine with a one-track mind. Make yourself more relatable by sharing something unexpected—a personal story or even details about a missed opportunity.

3. **Tame the timer.** Think about the way you set deadlines for your team. Are they perceived as reasonable? Or outrageous? When possible, slow down. And when situations emerge with tight time demands, you'll likely experience greater cooperation and better attitudes from your colleagues.

4. **Plug in to a new outlet.** Divert some of your abundant energy into a different direction. Get more involved with a professional organization or volunteer for community service, adding depth to a one-dimensional image. You'll also reap the emotional benefits of supporting a worthy cause.

5. **Just breathe.** Even when those around you operate at a slower pace, actively work to keep your frustration level in check. A deep breath and a smile can help to camouflage your impatience while you learn to temper your full-speed-ahead style.

Laura's Turnaround

In her usual fashion of pushing for continuous improvement in every aspect of her business, Laura brought me in as an executive coach to help enhance the company's leadership bench strength and improve her effectiveness as a leader. *Dust in My Wind* syndrome quickly emerged as the obvious blind spot affecting Laura, not to mention those who reported to her. I was excited to work with her, and I could tell that she would be eager to tackle the challenge ahead once she uncovered the blind spot for herself.

Early on, I asked Laura to reflect on some important questions:

- Just because I can do it, does it mean that everyone else can?
- Do I serve as an enviable role model or an unrealistic one?
- Is it fair to place the same "over the top" expectations on others that I set for myself?
- Am I creating an environment that promotes unhealthy competition instead of collaborative teamwork?

The process of self-reflection helped Laura to see that she might have some limiting beliefs surrounding this issue. Limiting beliefs typically stem from an event early in life that a person misinterprets and then considers to be true from that point forward. While Laura quickly admitted she had a strong work ethic, she tended to describe herself as being of average intelligence. I had to get Laura to recognize that she really *wasn't* average. Far from it. And given that, she needed to correct the false belief that most of her peers and colleagues could perform at her same capacity if only they tried.

> *Limiting beliefs:* thought processes that typically stem from an event early in life that a person misinterprets and then considers to be true from that point forward.

Initially, Laura was uncomfortable with the idea of "lowering her standards" and couldn't understand why the owner of a company should have to adjust deadlines and agendas. After we worked together and discussed the implications of this emotional barrier, Laura began to see that she sometimes needed to meet people where *they* are, not always where *she* is. Once she accepted that her own capabilities were much greater than others (okay, off the charts), she began to see the value in keeping her expectations and productivity demands in check. Due to her desire—her drive, if you will—to improve as a leader, Laura was committed to changing her perspective and creating more positive perceptions among her staff members.

Her new mission for behavior change helped Laura to become aware of subtle clues that she soon realized had been present for most of her career. Comments like, *"Laura, not everyone is like you,"* began to take on new meaning. The subtle clues then gave way to those that were much more overt. One of Laura's strongest leaders, a woman most saw as calm and poised, began to show clear signs of fatigue and breakdown. During one meeting, this respected leader began to cry when confronted with a simple question. Realizing that the stress of keeping up with her expectations was taking a toll, Laura canvassed others on her team to see if this reaction was an anomaly. Not surprisingly, she discovered that many of her staff members went through periods where the pressure made them feel high-strung, volatile, and much less composed—virtual powder kegs of unmitigated stress.

For Laura, the light bulb was turning on. She genuinely started to see the link between these responses and her highly ambitious demands. Once she truly understood her blind spot and reached a point of self-awareness, she was ready to take action to change the problem. What Laura needed most was someone who could hold up the virtual stop sign when her expectations were out of line. Laura let her *entire* staff know that this was an area she was truly committed to changing, and she asked for their collective help to alert her when she needed to slow down. Imagine the surprise and relief they all felt!

Because of Laura's changes, the employee turnover rate at her company dropped while productivity and staff morale hit an all-time high.

Laura must have made a fairly compelling and sincere case when asking for honest feedback. Her staff began to open up to her about needing more time to just "be" with their colleagues. They lamented that they never got a chance to gel as a team because of their packed agendas. They wanted more time to simply get better acquainted and discover how they could support each other more effectively. Some on her staff even admitted that they felt like every assignment was a contest to see who could make Laura most proud or impressed. Surely this was a real eye-opener for Laura, but she was ready to handle the feedback and do something about it.

Months later, Laura put her newfound self-awareness and insights on display for her employees in a rather stunning fashion. Instead of planning her traditional 14-hour, back-to-back strategy- and training-packed agenda for the annual corporate meeting, Laura presented a 20-minute, state-of-the-union speech that concluded with a heavily symbolic photo. The image showed a runner crossing the finish line, hands held high, while the runners trailing behind her look exhausted. She used this photo to further acknowledge her own shortcomings as a leader and ask for additional feedback to continue improving the morale of the team. As if that didn't shock the attendees enough, Laura then dismissed the staff for an afternoon of bowling and fun.

As you might guess, Laura's company experienced a number of changes since that surprising day that ended at the bowling lanes. Besides the lower employee turnover rate and greater productivity, staff morale hit an all-time high. Does Laura still occasionally slip into peak-velocity mode? Yes, she admits. But she's now built a level of credibility and rapport with her team members that allows them to openly communicate with her when the pace starts to feel frenetic.

"If there is any one secret of success, it lies in the ability to get the other person's point of view and see things from that person's angle as well as from your own."

HENRY FORD
(Founder of Ford Motor Company)

APPLIED SELF-AWARENESS

If *Dust in My Wind* syndrome appears to be your professional blind spot, try using these action items as a guide for change:

1 Take a close look at your thoughts and behaviors surrounding teamwork, goals and deadlines. Be honest about your tendencies and the pace that seems normal for you. How does that pace compare with your colleagues and co-workers? Any surprises?

My Action Items: _____

_____

_____

_____

_____

2 Examine your belief system and assumptions. Do you have a false sense of your own capabilities and capacity? Could you be more successful by updating your deeply entrenched thought processes with a fresh perspective?

My Action Items: _____

_____

_____

_____

3 Watch for clues (subtle and not-so-subtle) that indicate the people around you are getting tired and frustrated with the pace you are setting. Pay attention to words, body language, facial expressions, and tone of voice. Make this an ongoing process in your interactions with others.

My Action Items: _____

_____

_____

4 Ask for direct feedback about your leadership and interpersonal skills from colleagues you trust. Listen carefully and respectfully. Then use that input to adjust your behavior—and closely monitor the response.

My Action Items: _____

_____

_____

_____

5 Make the conscious commitment to slow down and meet people where they are (not always where you are). Integrate the feedback you've gained to improve your communication and your relationships.

My Action Items: _____

_____

_____

6 Admit your shortcomings as a team member or leader, and ask your colleagues for gentle reminders if they begin feeling too much pressure with the pace of work. Remind yourself that great ideas and groundbreaking innovations usually emerge when people have the time and mental space to think outside the box.

My Action Items: _____

_____

_____

_____

7 Recognize the talents and gifts of your co-workers, and express appreciation for their contributions. Working to strengthen team relationships will generate a wide range of benefits—for you and for the company.

My Action Items: _____

_____

_____

8 Don't be too hard on yourself. Remember that you have incredible talents and good intentions, and you're actively making the effort to improve your "delivery" of those qualities. Positive results are destined to follow.

My Action Items: _____

_____

_____

CHAPTER 6

No Crying in Baseball

Highly respected for his technical expertise, Reid held a top position in his company's IT department. He had a natural proclivity for all things relating to computers, including the calm demeanor to handle those IT problems that inevitably occur at the worst possible times. Software glitches. Equipment failures. Network outages.

While others reacted to an IT crisis with varying levels of panic, Reid was able to block out the frustration, identify the problem, and quickly implement a solution—usually without breaking a sweat. He was a master at keeping his composure even in the most intense situations. I'm quite sure that Reid would have been an excellent poker player.

When it was time for the company to incorporate new software and expand its growing data infrastructure, Reid was clearly the most qualified technical expert to lead the team project. He was intelligent, experienced and unflappable under pressure. So why were his supervisors uneasy about assigning him the task?

Some of the very attributes that made Reid an outstanding technical asset for the company also made him a liability in a leadership position. His staff members perceived him as aloof and emotionless. If they approached him with a minor problem or a major crisis, he had the same flat response. He didn't recognize (much less acknowledge) other people's feelings, leaving the impression that he was indifferent to their stress, fear or anger.

Reid's perceived lack of emotion was alienating his staff, as well as his colleagues and internal customers. What should have been a strong reputation for technical excellence had been diluted by his reputation for having a mechanical, detached personality. No wonder senior executives were concerned about Reid's ability to engage and motivate a team while implementing a critical company-wide initiative.

Perception Disconnect

Emotion in the workplace can be a tricky subject. In the 1992 hit movie, "A League of Their Own," Actor Tom Hanks played the part of a coach working in the first female professional baseball league. Expressing his disbelief and outrage at seeing a player's tears "on the job," Hanks delivered the film's classic line: *"There's no crying in baseball!"* Humor aside, that statement speaks volumes about a workplace norm embraced by many people in the corporate world, including Reid. They strongly believe that all emotions should be checked at the door when you arrive at the office. In Reid's case, that belief took on a life of its own and eventually created an icy barrier that was blocking his career advancement.

Reid's professional blind spot—what I call *No Crying in Baseball* syndrome—is often seen in those who have high cognitive intelligence but low emotional intelligence. People in this category excel at functional, task-related skills like technology or finance but fall short with things like relationship-building and empathy. That disparity might go unnoticed early on. But when people like Reid suddenly become stuck in their careers, unable to get the next promotion or convince a supervisor to give them more responsibility, the problem isn't linked to their tangible skills. In fact, those are often exemplary. The real culprit is their lack of intangible skills. They simply don't have an emotional connection with the people around them.

What should have been a strong reputation for technical excellence had been diluted by Reid's reputation for having a mechanical, detached personality.

To explain it another way, imagine how you might feel if you signed up to take a college course during a summer session. You have perfect attendance, complete every assignment and make the top scores in the class on each test. You anticipate a final grade of 98, which will be a nice boost for your GPA. But when your report card arrives, you are stunned to see that the registrar shows you enrolled in a second class you never attended and, obviously, received a 0. Semester average: 49. Ouch. Despite the 98 in the other class, the combined impact on your GPA is disastrous.

People with *No Crying in Baseball* syndrome are in exactly the same situation: they simply don't realize they are being graded in a separate discipline, one that is dragging down their overall value despite their brilliance in another area. A+ for Tangible Skills. D- for Intangible Skills. Once they actually understand and accept that concept, they can examine their stagnant career paths with a whole new layer of context and begin to identify why they have been struggling. They are often shocked to find out that their "corporate GPA" is much lower than they thought! Even if they perform their job-related tasks perfectly, they need to improve a different set of skills if they want to succeed.

For those with *No Crying in Baseball* syndrome, improving this new skill set involves changing negative perceptions—the unfortunate and unflattering impressions that were formed while they were unaware of being graded on another dimension of their performance. They may have seen themselves as focused and even-tempered, but the people around them had a vastly different perspective.

Composed and steady?

PERCEPTION GAP

Or robotic and indifferent?

Grasping this idea can be tough for people with *No Crying in Baseball* syndrome. It's a difficult blind spot to overcome, but also potentially the biggest detriment to career progress. That simply means you have a great opportunity to make a powerful change—one that is well worth the time and effort you invest in shifting your mindset and creating some new habits.

Even if people with *No Crying in Baseball* syndrome perform their job-related tasks perfectly, they need to improve a different set of skills if they want to succeed.

If you think you might have tendencies toward *No Crying in Baseball* syndrome, ask yourself these questions: Do you feel uncomfortable showing any kind of emotions at the office? Do you inwardly lose respect for colleagues who express emotion more openly? Do you focus so intently on a task that you lose sight of the people involved? If any of these ring a bell, don't panic. There are valid strategies to help you make changes.

Start by uncovering the genesis of your belief that displaying emotion is inappropriate. Just understanding why you feel this way could help you to adjust your thinking. If you were upset or angry as a child, did your parents send you to your room until you could join the rest of the family with a pleasant demeanor? Have other people in your life reinforced the message that showing emotions is bad or weak? Did you have a negative experience that conditioned you to be emotionless in front of others or to remain unresponsive when others display emotions? With a little thought, you may be able to identify the root of the problem.

Recognize that there is a difference between "don't bring your personal problems to work" and "don't bring your personality to work." Relax a little. Most of us spend at least half of our waking hours at the office, so it's important to connect with our co-workers and relate to them on a more meaningful level. If we limit every interaction to the business at hand, our colleagues can only relate to us in a one-dimensional way, like only having a single outlet plug. When we are willing to reveal a deeper side of ourselves—our interests, goals and struggles—we expand the opportunities for others to "plug in" to who we really are as a complete, multi-faceted person. Be yourself, and try to expand the ways that your co-workers can connect with you.

Resist the urge to get to the bottom of things at the top of every conversation. You may have a natural tendency to gather as much data as possible so you can accurately evaluate any situation. It's probably in your DNA. However, that approach creates an intimidating tone when applied to co-worker inter-actions. People with *No Crying in Baseball* syndrome usually start every hallway conversation, phone call and email with a question. Where's the report? Can you attend the meeting? Will the project be ready before the deadline? To change that habit, take a few extra seconds to greet other people and ask how they are doing. It may seem calculated or rehearsed at first, but it can go a long way toward softening your ultimate data-gathering mission.

Look for specific opportunities to build rapport with others, even if it means stepping out of your comfort zone. That requires opening up enough so that you can find common ground with the people around you. Try sharing a part of yourself that no one else at the office knows. Your love of John Grisham novels.

Your passion for trivia games. Your talent for making homemade pasta. Don't think anyone cares? You might be surprised. And, frankly, your assumption that no one cares is probably being interpreted as, "*I'm not interested in your stories, so why would you be interested in mine?*" Once you open up, your colleagues will likely reciprocate. They'll start to see you in a different light. And chances are, you'll discover things you have in common other than work. When we show an interest in our co-workers and seek to understand what drives them, we can begin to build working relationships that lead to stronger, more productive teamwork.

As with most things in life, remember that balance is the goal. The solution for *No Crying in Baseball* syndrome isn't just about showing more emotion. No one is suggesting that you cry regularly during staff meetings or provide your boss with lengthy updates about your family drama. There's a fine line between sharing appropriately in a human, compassionate way and…well, TMI. Save that for the therapist's couch. The key to success is finding the right balance for being perceived by those around you as warm and caring, as well as professional and focused.

When we show an interest in our co-workers and
seek to understand what drives them, we can begin to
build working relationships that lead to stronger,
more productive teamwork.

PERCEPTION 9-1-1

Five Fast Fixes for
No Crying in Baseball Syndrome

1. Unfreeze your face. That's right...smile! It's simple. It's free. And what a big difference it can make!

2. Challenge your "no emotion at work" paradigm. Showing some emotion in the workplace is not only acceptable today but also *valuable*. Remind yourself that outdated thought processes need to be upgraded, just like old technology. It's time to trade in your emotion-free VCR for a warm, friendly Blu-Ray player.

3. Be more transparent. When it's appropriate, begin conversations with colleagues by briefly discussing something *other than business*. Ask about their weekend. Tell them about a great restaurant you discovered.

4. Find new ways to "plug in." Challenge yourself over the next week to discover something you have in common (besides work) with three of your colleagues. Share. Listen. Repeat. It's easier than you might think!

5. Try a little team bonding. Spend some time with your staff members and colleagues in a casual setting outside of the office and get to know them better. Suggest a group outing for pizza or a party to watch the big game.

Reid's Reaction

Now back to our high-tech superstar. Reid and I met after one of his senior vice presidents recommended that he might benefit from some executive coaching. After a few conversations with Reid, I was fairly certain that his professional blind spot was *No Crying in Baseball* syndrome.

To continue my evaluation, I asked Reid to take an emotional intelligence test (specifically, the well-known Bar-On EQ-i® assessment). The results confirmed my suspicions. Reid's empathy score was below average, while his impulse control score was off the charts (meaning that he controlled his emotions much too tightly at all times). The variance in these two scores is highly correlated. Reid may have been an expert at staying cool under pressure, but others viewed him as emotionless. Plus, the idea of showing or receiving empathy made Reid extremely uncomfortable, so he avoided those situations by staying frozen within a very narrow band of responses and feelings. He was essentially protecting himself with "emotional Botox."

My first challenge was to find out why Reid felt so strongly about his total boycott on workplace emotion. As we talked, I discovered that he had a deeply ingrained belief that showing feelings of any type in the office is unprofessional and inappropriate behavior. That idea started with his father and was reinforced by several influential people throughout his career. I also began to wonder whether Reid was actively suppressing his emotions or if years of emotionless interactions had become second nature. Our discussions proved it was the latter. Reid viewed the world through a purely analytical, black-and-white lens that filtered out the colors and textures of feelings. He simply never saw things from an emotional perspective, and that made him seem unapproachable and distant.

Reid may have been an expert at staying cool under pressure, but others viewed him as emotionless. He was essentially protecting himself with "emotional Botox."

If you're familiar with the Myers-Briggs Personality Type Indicator, two profiles come to mind. Someone identified as a "Thinker" relies entirely on facts and figures for decision-making. In contrast, people with the "Feeler" personality type rely heavily on emotions and make decisions based on their impact for themselves and others. Reid was definitely all "Thinker," but he would need to seek greater balance if he wanted to get ahead.

To guide Reid down this path, I wanted to show him that his extremely logical approach to life left little room to factor in people. He needed to see concrete proof of how his emotionless disposition was affecting others. With his help, we gathered anonymous feedback from his staff members and colleagues, including specific examples of Reid's words, actions and body language that others perceived as uncaring or offensive. Just like our analogy about the student who discovered the second class on the report card, Reid was shocked by the results. He was completely unaware of the negative perceptions he was unintentionally forming.

Reid finally realized that he needed to make some changes, and he was highly motivated to get started. He asked for help to develop an action plan for integrating some of the "Feeler" personality traits into his staunchly "Thinker"-type demeanor. We talked at length about the signals he should watch for to help him identify the way others were feeling. To pick up on those subtle nuances of communication, he would need to tune in to the people around him at a higher frequency.

I asked Reid to put a huge question mark sign on his computer to secretly remind him that every conversation should not start with a probing, data-gathering question or request. I also encouraged him to consider the benefits of being more transparent, opening up about his own feelings and concerns so that his co-workers could connect with him on a more human level. I convinced him that showing a little bit of vulnerability would go a long way toward building rapport with his staff members.

To pick up on subtle nuances of communication, Reid would need to tune in to the people around him at a higher frequency.

Change didn't happen for Reid overnight, but he was happy to report on his progress in a recent coaching session. (He was even smiling!) During an informal meeting, he told his staff members a story about his hometown that he had never before shared with anyone in the office. To his utter surprise, his colleagues were interested and intrigued. One co-worker even stopped by his office later to ask a question about the story. This helped to form a foundation for a deeper connection that proved valuable on a subsequent project. That glimmer of success encouraged him to continue being more open, as well as showing a sincere interest in the multi-dimensional lives of the people around him.

Reid also formed a best practices group within his IT department, which enabled interaction for a professional purpose but also provided a regular opportunity to connect with the members on a more personal level. Once he could see the true impact, Reid became more skilled at infusing his previously rigid professional life with the softness of empathy and emotion. His career seemed back on track, and his mood was noticeably elevated.

"To handle yourself, use your head;
to handle others, use your heart."

ELEANOR ROOSEVELT
(Civil Rights Activist & Former U.S. First Lady)

APPLIED SELF-AWARENESS

If your professional blind spot might be *No Crying in Baseball,* these action items could help you make some positive changes:

1 Accept the idea that your work performance is being graded on two different levels (tangible and intangible). Then make the commitment to elevate the quality of your intangible skills so you can raise your "overall corporate GPA" and be better positioned to move your career forward.

My Action Items: _____

_____

_____

_____

2 Create a new strategy for interacting with the people around you. Start with a smile and a greeting, rather than a pointed question. Pay attention to what's going on around you, aside from your goal-intensive focus. Look beyond the processes to see the people involved.

My Action Items: _____

_____

_____

_____

3 Establish new daily goals designed to build relationships and form the foundation for stronger teamwork. Remind yourself that these are just as important as the functional/technical goals, and they might even be the key to greater productivity. Sure, you may be skeptical about the connection at first, but give it a try. You'll be pleasantly surprised!

My Action Items: _____

_____

_____

4 Strengthen your empathy muscle. Get in the habit of thinking about your words and actions in terms of the emotions they might generate with your colleagues. Will you likely make them feel reassured and confident or intimidated and defensive?

My Action Items: _____

_____

_____

_____

5 Open up and let your co-workers see your softer side. Showing a little emotion and vulnerability can make you more relatable, likable and successful.

My Action Items: _____

_____

_____

6 Post a sign or symbol on your desk as a constant reminder to use more conscious communication. This visual image will prompt you to choose words, tone of voice, and body language that create the new perception you want—warm, caring and personable.

My Action Items: _____

_____

_____

_____

7 Show a genuine interest in your colleagues—their unique talents, their hobbies and their families. Be willing to share some of your own personal facts, and look for things you have in common as a way to build stronger connections.

My Action Items: _____

_____

_____

_____

8 Respect the need for balance. Avoid the trap of trying to replace your complete no-emotion zone with an unlimited feelings free-for-all. Going too far in the other direction could definitely have negative results.

My Action Items: _____

_____

_____

_____

9 Ask for feedback from a few trusted co-workers to measure your progress over time. By their very nature, blind spots are hard to monitor. An objective evaluation from an outside source can be quite valuable as you develop and refine your new skill set.

My Action Items: _____

_____

_____

_____

CHAPTER 7

Safety Patrol

Paige worked for nearly a decade as a bank examiner, conducting independent audits for the Federal Reserve at selected banks throughout the country. With her analytical slant, she excelled at monitoring, assessing and evaluating companies based on their compliance with applicable laws and financial regulations. Paige was known for precisely following policies and procedures, and she was very thorough at helping to ensure that others did as well. Her supervisors knew she would leave no stone unturned.

While visiting other companies, Paige was accepted as an outside expert and candidly informed the bank administrators about compliance gaps and omissions. No sugar coating. No softening the blow. If there was a problem, Paige pointed it out.

The companies were required to make the changes, and then Paige was out the door and on to the next bank.

Paige was eventually hired to lead the compliance department at one of the banks she had previously audited. Although she got very little resistance as a visiting bank examiner, she discovered that her advice as an in-house employee was met with a remarkably different attitude. Paige was now in enemy territory. As if being part of the audit team didn't carry enough stigma, her cut-and-dried approach to finding errors created a prickly perception that wasn't doing her any favors. She could no longer make a quick exit after identifying the potential pitfalls in the bank's business model and processes. It soon became clear that relationship building was not among the many skills she had gained during her impressive financial career.

As if being part of the audit team didn't carry enough stigma, Paige's cut-and-dried approach to finding errors created a prickly perception that wasn't doing her any favors.

To her co-workers, Paige's constant identification of the risks sounded like the voice of doom. Managers would bristle at the idea of having Paige review their departments' practices. Her operational colleagues felt that she simply didn't empathize with the time and cost involved in ensuring the company complied with each and every industry regulation. If there was an innovative idea, Paige provided 10 reasons why it wouldn't work. If someone suggested a new process, Paige explained how it would need to comply with the company regulations. Even though Paige had a relatively optimistic outlook on many areas of her life, her colleagues and co-workers only saw the "glass half empty" person who zoomed in on problems and always played by the rules.

Paige definitely brought the bank a wealth of information and helped them avoid potential fines, but she seemed unable to position her knowledge within the context of the bank's operations.

The bank executives who had been so excited about bringing Paige on board were now getting anxious—and having second thoughts. Paige definitely brought them a wealth of information and helped them avoid potential fines, but she seemed unable to position her knowledge within the context of the bank's operations. She also wasn't making any progress to reduce the already-strong resistance facing the audit team as a whole. That disconnect was preventing them from taking full advantage of her compliance expertise.

Perception Disconnect

In many elementary schools, the oldest students dream of receiving a prestigious honor: being selected for the school Safety Patrol. Membership in this elite group is reserved only for those who demonstrate the highest levels of maturity and responsibility (well, as much as you could realistically have at age 10 or 11). Decked out in their official Safety Patrol vests, these trusted students take their jobs very seriously. Boldly stopping traffic so that their classmates can safely cross. Carefully making sure everyone arrived on the other side. Signaling the cars to proceed again with a friendly yet authoritative nod. Yes, the Safety Patrol members are there on the front line, proudly protecting everyone from the traffic dangers that lurk on the outskirts of the playground area.

Paige and those who share her tendency to see potential disaster at every turn have what I refer to as *Safety Patrol* syndrome. These folks are just wired to point out possible risks and hazards. It's simply how they view situations and opportunities, often not even aware of the negative slant. From their perspective, they have the responsibility to keep everyone from making a mistake or forgetting an important guideline. It's an honorable duty for them, and they sincerely approach it with care and concern. But here's the problem. People with *Safety Patrol* syndrome seem to live in a purely black-and-white world, rigidly conforming to rules and regulations regardless of the circumstances. They worry incessantly about the potential pitfalls of new ideas, stifling creativity like the proverbial wet blanket. Without the flexibility to think outside the lines (at least in some cases), they become known as the always-unwelcome rain on their co-workers' parade.

To her co-workers, Paige's constant identification
of the risks sounded like the voice of doom.

Before we continue, let me point out that every company does indeed need people who can analyze situations, identify possible problems and associated risks, and keep great ideas grounded in realistic parameters. The issue here is *how* they apply those skills. Without attention to things like timing, delivery and tone, the people frequently responsible for sharing bad news can quickly develop a reputation as being negative or even toxic.

Ask about this issue at any company, and employees can easily pinpoint the person who has *Safety Patrol* syndrome. But, like many of the professional blind spots, those who suffer from the syndrome often find it quite difficult to recognize. They see themselves as realistic and practical. They aren't deliberately trying to be adversarial and, in fact, often see themselves as providing a valuable service. They have a tangible skill for identifying problems and rapidly determining the fastest, most efficient solution. Unfortunately, the people around them have a very different perception.

Methodical and compliant?

PERCEPTION GAP

Or inflexible and overly cautious?

At this point, you may be thinking of someone in your office who is regularly sporting the *Safety Patrol* vest—or perhaps that person is you. Consider the answers to these questions to help you determine if you might fit the role of cautious crossing guard more than you'd really prefer to admit. Do you find yourself looking for the problems or loopholes in every new idea? Do you frequently focus in on compliance hitches before getting the full story? Does it seem like your co-workers hold their breath whenever you provide a comment or critique in meetings? Do you follow rules and regulations in all situations, even when there are extenuating circumstances? If *Safety Patrol* syndrome could be your professional blind spot, here are a few suggestions to help you break out of that behavior pattern and begin to show colleagues your brighter side.

When colleagues are presenting ideas, get in the habit of gathering all of the facts before you verbalize any objections or even let your mind start racing ahead with its critical analysis. Pay attention. Listen closely. Then try to evaluate the ideas in a balanced, objective way. The most important thing is resisting the urge to point out the obstacles immediately and waiting to respond until you have considered the proposed concept in context.

Try to be more selective about when you raise the red flag on an idea. Pick your battles, as they say. When a situation arises that is truly worthy of sounding the alarm, your message will have more impact if it's not perceived as simply the latest warning in a long line of constant objections.

Accentuate the positive when you can. Admittedly, that will go against your nature. You have the ability to detect errors, shortcomings and drawbacks like a heat-seeking missile. That's a real talent. But when dealing with people, it can leave them feeling defensive and inadequate while making you look judgmental and downright grumpy. Force yourself to look for positive elements. Even if you still have to vote "no" on the issue at hand, you'll appear more objective if you can acknowledge the pros and cons. And in the process, you might find a compromise that makes everyone happy.

Regularly test your worst-case-scenario theories. Explore the possible outcomes: what's the worst that could happen if I don't object and we move forward with this idea? What is the cost of the risk versus the cost of *mitigating* the risk? You might discover that the time and money required to follow every policy and procedure to the letter are higher than the cost of handling a worst-case situation that likely won't even occur.

You can make a dramatic change in the way others perceive your feedback if you are offering cooperative compromises rather than condemnation.

Put your analytical, problem-solving expertise to work for a different cause. Challenge yourself to think of new solutions that incorporate innovative ideas within the boundaries of the rules and regulations you feel so compelled to protect. You can make a dramatic change in the way others perceive your feedback if you are offering cooperative compromises rather than condemnation. You might have to shift your mindset a bit from left brain to right brain and actually—*brace yourself!*—get creative. Don't let that intimidate you. Identifying a brilliant compromise is a quick way to go from zero to hero among your peers, and you have just the right brainpower to do it.

Recognize that your contribution to a team effort will be far more powerful if you master the art of influence. In other words, give your intangible skills just as much emphasis as your tangible skills. Here's why… The way you alert, inform or call attention to certain matters can be far more impactful than the matters themselves. If you have valuable information to share but others perceive that your ideas are presented as superior or non-negotiable, the intrinsic value you offer may be lost in a sea of resentment. Think about your word choices, your tone and your body language as you interact with others. When you enhance your ability to influence and persuade, you'll increase your credibility and start to change the way your co-workers react to and receive your opinions.

Recognize that your contribution to a team effort will be far more powerful if you master the art of influence. In other words, give your intangible skills just as much emphasis as your tangible skills.

PERCEPTION 9-1-1

Five Fast Fixes for
Safety Patrol Syndrome

1. **Focus on solutions.** Instead of simply telling others about the regulations, find options to help them comply with the rules while achieving their own goals. That approach will put you on the fast track to hero status among your colleagues.

2. **Resist the urge to fix everything.** Make sure criticism isn't always the first thing out of your mouth. Continuous improvement is an admirable goal, but immediately pointing out shortcomings to everyone in your path will have your co-workers running for cover behind their desks.

3. **Adopt the phrase, "What if...."** Remember that innovation and compliance *can* co-exist. Give your brain permission to color outside the lines a bit, and apply your unique problem-solving skills toward finding a smart compromise.

4. **Think dollars and sense.** Does it make sense to spend money on complying with certain regulations? What's the potential expense or advantage if you don't? A little cost/benefit analysis could add a big splash of perspective.

5. **Unleash the kinder, gentler you.** If you do have to point out negatives, focus on the problem instead of the people involved. Keep in mind that you and your colleagues are working toward a common goal, not engaging in warfare.

Paige's Predicament

Paige had only been in her new leadership position for three months, but her supervisor at the bank was able to help her recognize that her behavior was causing significant friction with her co-workers. She had quickly been tagged as the *Safety Patrol* member within the workplace. When I began to work with Paige, she was understandably frustrated and confused. My goal was to give her some specific strategies that would help her change the behaviors that were creating negative perceptions among her colleagues.

As we talked, Paige described her struggles to engage in strategy and brainstorming meetings with her peers. While she tried not to point out every single potential risk and concern, she wasn't always successful. She just couldn't help herself. Paige clearly felt a sincere responsibility to play the role of devil's advocate, and she hadn't yet made the mental adjustment to participating in a team context.

I asked Paige to shift the way she defined her job description. Instead of seeing herself as the "compliance queen," I challenged her to reframe the position as a compliance application specialist—someone who specializes in helping colleagues find a way to comply with regulations while minimizing disruption to their departments and operations. Whenever her natural tendency emerged to build a case against a new idea, she should replace that effort with something different: building rapport with her colleagues to find an appropriate compromise.

It took some time for Paige to get comfortable with the new thought process and the behaviors that supported it, but she made steady progress. She forced herself to look at how she could help others comply before she advised and warned them about a particular regulation. She began considering the direct and indirect costs associated with mitigating every possible risk, which allowed her to be more selective when sounding the alarm. She demonstrated balance when she showed sensitivity to the financial and human impact of the decision-making process. When she stopped providing the endless stream of warnings about rules and regulations, her co-workers actually began to listen to her comments and respect her opinions.

Slowly but surely, Paige was able to rebuild her reputation and regain the credibility she lost during her rocky start at the bank. By mastering the art of influence and improving her emotional intelligence, Paige's expertise was able to shine through and attract attention in a positive way. She learned to collaborate with her colleagues effectively and develop stronger solutions as a genuine part of her team.

"One who is constantly raising points of order and insisting upon a strict observance of every rule...makes himself a nuisance."

BRIG. GEN. HENRY MARTYN ROBERT
(Creator of "Robert's Rules of Order")

APPLIED SELF-AWARENESS

If your professional blind spot might be *Safety Patrol* syndrome, you may find these action items helpful:

1 Spend as much time thinking about *how* you can help others comply with rules and regulations as you do simply pointing them out. That will provide balance and better position your expertise as an asset to your colleagues and co-workers.

My Action Items: _____

_____

_____

_____

_____

2 Strive for balance in your analysis of new ideas or processes. Acknowledge the pros and cons, and build your credibility by limiting the number of times you sound the potential non-compliance alarm.

My Action Items: _____

_____

_____

_____

_____

3 Remember that it's not always your job to play devil's advocate. Ask yourself honestly: do I really believe this is a dangerous decision or do I like the challenge of winning the next battle? If I do support the decision, what's the worst thing that could happen?

My Action Items: _____

_____

_____

_____

4 Estimate the costs and benefits of the decision at hand. Most corporate success stories have involved accepting some level of risk, so consider the potential advantages that could result from taking a leap of faith.

My Action Items: _____

_____

_____

5 Remind yourself that you are operating in a team context. You and your colleagues are on the same side, so focus your energy on finding win/win solutions that allow you to reach your common goals.

My Action Items: _____

_____

_____

_____

6 Take steps to build better relationships with your colleagues. Open the lines of communication, and try to connect with them on a deeper level. Creating that rapport will provide a foundation for stronger collaboration.

My Action Items: _____

_____

_____

7 Dedicate more time to the art of influence and persuasion. The way that you present your point of view—your words, tone and body language—has an enormous impact on the way others perceive your message.

My Action Items: _____

_____

_____

_____

8 Harness your problem-solving expertise to look for realistic compromises. Take the lead in suggesting potential alternatives instead of just pointing out risks.

My Action Items: _____

_____

_____

_____

CHAPTER 8

Faulty Volume Control

Graham was in his final semester of an MBA program at a prominent university. As he prepared to leverage his graduate credentials, he was brimming with potential and ready to launch what was certain to be a promising career. Perfect GPA from a top-ranked school? Check. International internship? Check. Glowing recommendations? Check. No wonder Graham seemed to carry himself with a quiet confidence. As soon as he had that diploma in his hand, the employment offers would surely be pouring in. Or at least that was his theory.

Perhaps there was a hitch. Graham had always believed that it was impolite to "toot his own horn." Verbally promoting his strengths to others felt undignified and overbearing. Besides, his world-class resume spoke for itself and, without a doubt, Graham looked great on paper. If people asked him to explain his skills and capabilities, his awkward response left them with the impression that he might actually be offended by the request. His accomplishments were impressive. Period. End of story. Really, what's left to discuss?

Graham had always believed that it was impolite to "toot his own horn." Verbally promoting his strengths to others felt undignified and overbearing.

Traversing the halls of the same business building on campus was another MBA candidate named Kyle, a high-energy student who was armed with big credentials and a big personality to match. Just like Graham, Kyle was sporting a jaunty resume, but he clearly had a very different outlook on the concept of self-promotion. Unabashedly, he took advantage of every possible opportunity (even the less-than-appropriate ones) to tell anyone who would listen about his latest achievements.

Kyle celebrated every personal success with an all-out, no-holds-barred mission to spread the good news. We're talking about effusive email blasts and Facebook posts. Enthusiastic recaps for co-workers during brief elevator rides. Announcements to acquaintances in the produce aisle at the grocery store. As you might imagine, Kyle's self-promotion became a running joke for many of his fellow students. Extremely qualified, yet extremely annoying.

> Kyle celebrated every personal success with an all-out, no-holds-barred mission to spread the good news.

Perception Disconnect

Graham and Kyle may have vastly different personalities, but they share the same professional blind spot. These students have what I call *Faulty Volume Control.* Essentially, they are both struggling to find the optimal sound level for their own self-promotion. Graham's volume is soft enough to mimic the mute button, while Kyle's volume is cranked up to the level of full-throttle eardrum bursting. Fabulous resumes aside, these gentlemen won't be able to reach their full potential until they tune in and find just the right volume level for communicating their unique value propositions.

If you think about the volume control on your radio or iPod, the dial offers you a full range of sound levels—not an on/off switch limited to two choices. So if your current self-promotion is at Level 1, the solution isn't automatically jumping up to a 10. The goal is to find the right level for your specific situation. Most of the time, that perfect balance is somewhere in the middle.

By keeping your self-promotion level too low, you may be missing opportunities to strengthen your perceived value. In our highly competitive business world, potential employers receive an endless stream of spectacular resumes. What should be eye-catching highlights become interchangeable when so many applicants have outstanding grades, elite awards and solid experience. Today, if you expect your resume to be your one and only sales tool (no matter how impressive), you run the risk of getting lost in the crowd. It's a one-dimensional appeal that...well, falls flat. Getting hired or promoted is currently determined much less by what's on paper and much more by how you bring those credentials to life. Making yourself stand out involves turning up the volume—strategically sharing your strengths with the right people and infusing your personality to add warmth, depth and dimension to your resume.

Graham and Kyle won't be able to reach their full potential until they tune in and find just the right volume level for communicating their unique value propositions.

If your self-promotion volume control is frequently turned up to the highest level, the lesson here is that louder isn't always better. You might be diminishing your value and distracting from your credentials by interjecting a personal sales pitch into every interaction. The incessant promotion can irritate the people around you, eventually leading them to block out or discount anything you say. They begin to think of you as a mind-numbing, bone-jarring rock concert, and they learn to use earplugs for every performance. Should you remain completely silent during the next team meeting or group project? No. But you'd be wise to turn down the volume and add some finesse to your contributions.

Faulty Volume Control isn't simply a blind spot that hinders

MBA students eagerly trying to snag those first jobs with Fortune 500 companies. It also affects entry-level workers, mid-level managers and senior executives who are angling for that next promotion or lucrative stock option package. In fact, this blind spot might be even more problematic for those hoping to move up within the same company. They typically aren't submitting new resumes to the decision makers, so their perceived value is graded solely on their ability to share their strengths and accomplishments with the right people in a tactful, appropriate way. Whether they succeed or fail is often determined by whether they can find the right volume level and control the way their self-promotion is perceived.

Volume Too Low:
Understated and humble?
Or bland and forgettable?

PERCEPTION GAP

Volume Too High:
Assertive and enthusiastic?
Or self-serving and inappropriate?

Graham and Kyle may be extreme examples of the *Faulty Volume Control* syndrome, but you probably identify with one of them more than the other. What does that say about your volume level and your natural tendencies to communicate your own value? How do you think you are perceived by your colleagues, co-workers or fellow students when it comes to self-promotion?

Do you assume that everyone around you is already familiar with your achievements? Or do you tend to broadcast every step of your progress far and wide? Perhaps you are somewhere in between, but it is worth a closer look to determine whether your level is still too soft or too loud. If your volume control dial isn't at the optimal spot, you could be missing out on great opportunities or undermining your own success.

Volume Too Low

For those of you who prefer to whisper rather than scream your value, try to uncover the reasons behind that tendency. Can you identify a specific incident in your past when self-promotion generated a negative response? Or were there important people in your life who influenced you to adopt this pattern of communication? Sometimes analyzing the cause of a particular behavior can give you the facts you need (and permission) to make important changes.

The points of differentiation between people in terms of functional/technical skills have become extraordinarily narrow. To be distinct, we have to show people exactly *how* we bring those skills to the table and display the passion behind what we do. To turn up the volume on your self-promotion, try moving beyond "what" to "how" as you share your value. Your resume may list what you've done, but people really want to know how you did it. How did you generate your results? How do you relate to other people on your team? How do you perform in leadership roles? How do you respond to adversity?

Remember that self-promotion is an ongoing task, even if you work in the same office for years. Long ago, it was fairly common to have the same boss for decades. Today, managers come and go—and with each one, we face the task of educating that new supervisor about our work and our areas of specialization. The competition continues, and we can no longer identify ourselves long-term with our companies or employers. That's precisely why we've seen explosive growth in the concept of Personal Branding in recent years. We are each individuals with unique features and benefits that employers could leverage for a competitive advantage. If we don't actively "sell" those distinctions, we disappear into the endless line of indistinguishable people with impressive resumes who are vying for the same title or corner office. For those who want to move ahead or, sadly, even keep their current jobs, self-promotion needs to become a recurring theme.

To turn up the volume on your self-promotion,
try moving beyond "what" to "how"
as you share your value.

Don't surrender to the idea that you have no control over how someone evaluates you and your work. Start to think about yourself as an influencer, as active rather than passive. Imagine that you are the director, transforming the words on your resume into a riveting, 3-D movie that gets rave reviews. Yes, it helps if you start with a good script, but the way you animate those words will determine your success. You can demonstrate that your resume is only one facet of your overall value by looking for smart opportunities to display your personality and verbalize your strengths. You have more control than you might think, so use that power to bring your value proposition to life in a credible and influential manner.

One way to increase your volume level without going overboard is to use stories that highlight your skills and talents. Your message will feel more understated when it's tucked carefully inside your example, but it will actually have greater impact by showing your knowledge and resourcefulness in action. For instance, you don't need to announce to your team that you can save the day because you know the required software program better than anyone on the planet. Instead, you could explain a similar challenge that came up last year and describe how you were able to successfully use that program to get the desired results for the team. At the end, they'll still know you are an expert but the perception will be quite different.

Despite realizing the need for louder self-promotion, some "Volume Too Low" people still find it difficult to venture out of their introverted comfort zones. It takes time to move in that direction, so keep trying and celebrate the small steps forward. You also have another option. Find a mentor or advocate who clearly knows your strengths and is willing to champion you in the right circles. An influential supporter can nominate you for awards or make sure your name is included when promotions or bonuses are being considered. You still want to grow in terms of communicating your value, but a persuasive mentor can supplement your efforts in a significant way.

Volume Too High

If you fall into the "Volume Too High" group, you probably enjoy sharing information with the people around you and feel totally comfortable pointing out your own assets. Is that just your personality? Have you been rewarded for "selling your value" in the past? Or were you overlooked for a major promotion by remaining silent? Perhaps you worked with or for people who weren't very good at self-promotion, and those are the only examples you've had to follow. Whatever the impetus, it's always helpful to understand why you keep your sales volume on high.

Sometimes less really is more. If you are continually attacking people with your value message, they likely have one goal: getting out of your way. Listening to you ceases to be an option. Chances are, this habit is deeply embedded, and you may not even realize you are doing it. Your first task is to raise your awareness. Think before you speak, and try to evaluate how your words will be perceived. Are you sharing important information or calling unnecessary attention to your latest corporate victory? Too much self-promotion can work against you, so pay attention and make a conscious effort to dial it back.

As a gentle reminder, you might want to leave yourself some unobtrusive signs to help jog your memory. Try writing the word "volume" on several post-it notes and placing them on your desk or in your wallet. It's a simple signal, but it might prevent you from falling into old patterns of blaring your benefits.

Too much self-promotion can work against you, so pay attention and make a conscious effort to dial it back.

Several of the strategies used for the low end of *Faulty Volume Control* also work well for those on the opposite side. Encasing your value message in a pertinent story will keep it grounded in purpose and not simply floating around aimlessly. The key for you is ensuring that the stories you tell are relevant in the current conversation. You could also gain an edge by finding a mentor who understands your value and is willing to communicate it. Your message could get a huge shot of credibility when it comes from the mouth of an ally instead of your own.

Because of your louder approach to self-promotion, others may perceive you as less of a team player. No matter how brilliant you are, nobody wants to work with someone who seems to be fearlessly "out for #1" at all times. To change that, you'll want to shift your thinking and your conversations from "I" to "we." Talk in terms of team goals, department progress and group success. While it might seem somewhat counterintuitive, you may be able to boost your own personal value by demonstrating that you have the capacity to share the spotlight.

Give that new teamwork attitude some real traction. Take the next step toward building relationships with your co-workers and colleagues in different ways. One of the most important things you can do is listen. When you are singularly focused on talking, selling yourself, or thinking about whatever you want to say next, you aren't paying sincere attention to the people around you. That means you are missing out on opportunities to connect with them and identify common ground. Focus outward. Actively look for value in others and take the time to acknowledge it. When you can demonstrate that you are listening to them, they may be able to stop blocking you out and begin hearing your message.

PERCEPTION 9-1-1

Five Fast Fixes for
Faulty Volume Control Syndrome

1. Give yourself the Goldilocks test. Take an honest look at the way you broadcast your strengths and skills. Is your level of self-promotion too soft, too loud or just right? It's time to start moving in the proper direction.

2. Schedule a regular "sound check." As you make changes, check to see if your adjustments are getting the results you want. If your self-promotion continues to be on the soft side, crank up the volume a bit. If you're still blaring, tone it down.

3. Write your own slogan. In other words, crystallize your value proposition—your unique advantages—so you can be ready to communicate them easily when a great opportunity arises. No stumbling for words, no rambling for hours.

4. Register for Storytelling 101. Weave your accomplishments and strengths into a pertinent story to make them shine through with sparkling credibility. When you give your success some context, it will sound believable rather than boastful.

5. Try a dress rehearsal. It can feel awkward at first to promote yourself in a different way, so practice telling your story out loud with a family member or close friend. Rehearsing will help you feel more prepared to communicate your personal value—and you never know when you might end up sitting next to the CEO in the corporate cafeteria.

The Volume Intervention

I became acquainted with Graham and Kyle when I was hired by their university to coach its MBA students. Both of these young men had great potential, but the contrast between their approaches was particularly striking. They were demonstrating the blind spot of *Faulty Volume Control* at both extremes of the spectrum. My goal was to provide strategies that would help each one of these students reach a more successful level of self-promotion.

With Graham, I knew my challenge would be recalibrating his thought process about sharing his value with others. As we talked, I discovered that his mother and grandmother had told him for years that it was inappropriate and unacceptable to "toot your own horn." Anything that even remotely sounded like bragging was a punishable offense in his house. To compensate, Graham invested countless hours in building a resume that would presumably remove all doubt about his qualifications without requiring him to say a single word.

I reminded Graham that the people from older generations who perpetuated the unequivocal ban on horn-tooting were not faced with the same challenges we have today. It's a different world now, with a brand new set of rules. I encouraged Graham to give up the idea that self-promotion is wrong or disgraceful. *It's necessary.* We have to be proactive in seizing opportunities to showcase our value if we want to succeed, and there are plenty of tactful, gracious ways to go about it. Once Graham accepted the evolution of self-promotion and the new requirements, he stopped feeling guilty about the idea of verbally communicating his value.

Since this was a new arena for Graham, I helped him to formulate some short, impactful stories that he could use to illustrate his talents in a meaningful yet modest way. Pre-packaged and ready to use, these stories allowed Graham to begin stepping out of his comfort zone and turning up his self-promotion volume. Graham also mentioned that he had been working closely with a particular professor in his MBA program. I suggested that he should continue forging that bond and tap into the relationship for brainstorming about additional ways to enhance his marketability. That professor ultimately recommended Graham for a prestigious achievement award and wrote him a stellar recommendation after he graduated.

We have to be proactive in seizing opportunities to showcase our value if we want to succeed, and there are plenty of tactful, gracious ways to go about it.

During my time working with Kyle, we discussed the ramifications of overzealous self-promotion and the hazards of being perceived as conceited. We explored whether his approach might stem from a scarcity mentality and a sense of desperation—the fear that there might not be enough success or work to go around. That seemed to strike a nerve. Through our conversations, Kyle started to realize that his never-ending sales pitch was hurting (not helping) his case. He also began to understand the gap between his intended communications and the way they were actually perceived by those around him. At that point, Kyle was ready to implement the strategies necessary to help him close the gap.

I encouraged Kyle to formulate some stories that could carry his value message and deliver it in a less obtrusive manner. We talked about using tact and diplomacy when sharing information, and we used some role-playing exercises to experiment with different scenarios. Kyle quickly learned that he needed to stick to the script and be cautious about his timing. Applying his usual eager attitude, he began implementing this approach and was thrilled (perhaps amazed) at the different reactions and responses he received. In fact, one of the department heads he assisted part-time eventually took notice of Kyle's more sophisticated use of self-promotion and turned out to be a tremendous asset in his post-graduation job hunt.

Kyle realized that empathy and tuning in to his colleagues' feelings would provide him with the perfect guide in his quest to find the right volume level for his personal self-promotion.

One of the most important things I pointed out to Kyle was based on my favorite quote from Poet Maya Angelou: "*People will forget what you said, people will forget what you did, but people will never forget how you made them feel.*" I asked Kyle, above all else, to pay close attention to the way he makes other people feel when he is in their presence. This was a new perspective for Kyle, but I hoped it would prompt him to mentally ask some tough questions: Am I making these people feel comfortable and appreciated? Or do they seem to be apathetic? Worse yet, annoyed?

If others perceived that Kyle was only interested in himself and his own accomplishments, they would naturally assume he didn't care about them at all. The greatest resume in the world couldn't possibly counteract that negative perception. Kyle soon realized that empathy and tuning in to his colleagues' feelings would provide him with the perfect guide in his quest to find the right volume level for his personal self-promotion.

Since completing their MBAs, Graham and Kyle have both made their way quite successfully in corporate America. With practice, they each learned how to counteract their natural self-promotion tendencies and found the optimal volume level for communicating their equally impressive value propositions.

"If you don't get noticed, you don't have anything. You just have to be noticed, but the art is in getting noticed naturally, without screaming or without tricks."

LEO BURNETT
(World-Famous Advertising Executive)

APPLIED SELF-AWARENESS

If your professional blind spot might be *Faulty Volume Control*, you may find these action items helpful:

Faulty Volume Control: Too Low

1 Challenge your belief that self-promotion is boastful. Times have changed, and communicating your value is now a necessity—not a social faux pas. Your success depends on changing that fundamental attitude.

My Action Items: _____

_____

_____

_____

2 Remember that your resume is only one facet of your qualifications for a job. The other facets—things like your ability to work with others, build rapport and lead effectively—won't show up on paper. The only way to communicate those strengths is by learning to speak up and promote your full value to the people who matter.

My Action Items: _____

_____

_____

_____

3 Get clarity on your value proposition. You'll feel more prepared to insert your message at the right time if you've thought about it in advance and collected the best words to describe your unique advantages.

My Action Items: _____

_____

_____

4 Give your accomplishments context and credibility by weaving them into a story. This will help you move beyond sharing what you did to showing how you did it.

My Action Items: _____

_____

_____

_____

5 Practice communicating your message in front of a friend to boost your comfort level—or try it out at your next networking event. You'll begin to see that it's possible to promote yourself politely and gracefully with sophistication.

My Action Items: _____

_____

_____

_____

6 Find an advocate who knows your talents and is willing to support your career advancement. Adding a second voice is a great way to turn up the volume on your self-promotion.

My Action Items: _____

_____

_____

7 Remind yourself that you could be missing out on great opportunities if you don't actively increase the level of your self-promotion. Many people around you are quite willing to share their stories, so it's critical for you to push your boundaries if you want to compete effectively.

My Action Items: _____

_____

_____

8 Make self-promotion an ongoing project. Just because you land the new job or get the big bonus doesn't mean you can stop communicating your value. You never know what's ahead, so keep sharing your story whenever you get the chance.

My Action Items: _____

_____

_____

_____

Faulty Volume Control: Too High

1 Recognize that you could be undermining your own success by hitting people over the head with your self-promotion. It's probably a habit, but you can break it.

My Action Items: _____

_____

_____

_____

2 Compress your value proposition into its most compact form. When your main message is ready in a short, succinct package, you'll be less tempted to use rambling descriptions that cause co-workers to tune out.

My Action Items: _____

_____

_____

3 Try folding your value message into a story that conveys your strengths in a more memorable and impactful way.

My Action Items: _____

_____

_____

_____

4 Pause before you launch into a self-promoting story. How is your message likely to be perceived in this situation? Is it the right time or is it a stretch? The goal is to be diplomatic and tactful. It should feel authentic, not forced.

My Action Items: _____

_____

_____

_____

5 Listen. And keep listening. When you are busy talking about yourself, you can't learn about others. That prevents you from building relationships and finding new ways to connect with those around you.

My Action Items: _____

_____

_____

6 Funnel your natural enthusiasm into a different path. Instead of singing your own praises, use that energy to broadcast the success of your team or a well-deserved colleague. Sharing the limelight could have a surprisingly positive impact on you.

My Action Items: _____

_____

_____

7 Find a believable mentor who will champion your work. Messages about your accomplishments may have more credibility if they come from an independent source.

My Action Items: _____

_____

_____

_____

8 Remember that self-promotion isn't just about providing reams of your personal information to others; it's about how you make them feel. When in doubt about what to share or when, strive to leave the perception that you care about others and what's important to them.

My Action Items: _____

_____

_____

_____

_____

CHAPTER 9

Passion Pistol

Corey was known for her strong sense of determination and spunky enthusiasm. She was charismatic, witty and effortlessly likeable. Despite growing up in less-than-ideal circumstances, she pushed past a wide range of challenges to create a life that sounded like something from a novel about the great American dream. She patched together loans, scholarships and part-time jobs to put herself through college, working tediously long hours to earn her degree. After emerging as a top performer in her first job at a call center, Corey recognized that she had a natural talent for sales, as well as teaching and mentoring others. She used that expertise in her next position, successfully designing and delivering training courses on sales and leadership.

Corey's career progressed rapidly with an executive position at a large insurance firm and later as a Regional Sales Manager for a national cable company. In each of these positions, Corey was brilliant in coaching her teams and helping them to refine their business and interpersonal skills—knowing when to push forward or pull back to maximize their sales. Her teams typically exceeded their performance goals and regularly had the lowest turnover rates in the company.

People loved working for Corey. *And why not?* She protected them like an anxious mother bear, funneling her boundless energy into guarding them from the predators of the corporate forest—layoffs, budget cuts, undesirable projects. Needless to say, she received exceptional reviews from her subordinates. Her supervisors and members of the executive team didn't always share that perspective.

As you might guess, Corey felt completely blindsided in a performance review when her boss suggested that she should curb her enthusiasm during interdepartmental meetings. He tactfully shared with her that the other department managers and several executives were becoming annoyed with her constant role as the super-charged advocate. According to some people, Corey seemed to be overly eager (and relentlessly vocal) when representing her team, her ideas or her projects. Her boss suggested that this unbridled exuberance might be diminishing her leadership presence.

Surely these comments were a mistake, she thought. Corey had always been praised and admired for her enthusiasm. *It was her trademark.* Couldn't they see that she was just being the strongest possible champion for the projects she cared about and the people who depended on her? Although she could be a bit of an evangelist at times, her intentions were nothing but honorable.

Perception Disconnect

Without question, Corey had a heartfelt passion for her job, her company and (perhaps most of all) the people she led. Her energy and enthusiasm were primary factors in helping her land previous jobs and earn promotions, but now they seemed to be creating a major roadblock. Corey suffers from what I call *Passion Pistol* syndrome. People who have this professional blind spot struggle with finding the proper way to apply their double-barreled enthusiasm. They've frequently been rewarded for this attribute in the past, so they don't always notice when it starts to misfire. In Corey's case, she unknowingly moved from carefully targeted shots of enthusiasm to rapid-fire blasts. No matter what she intended, she was sometimes perceived as overly intense.

People who have this professional blind spot struggle with finding the proper way to apply their double-barreled enthusiasm.

For people with *Passion Pistol* syndrome, the answer isn't simply about "dialing it back" and trying to implement a less-is-more philosophy. That's part of it, but certainly not the whole story. The bigger issue is about understanding exactly when it's appropriate to unleash those enthusiasm bullets. Consider this example. Every Fourth of July, many of us look forward to watching the patriotic fireworks displays. It's a time-honored tradition to *ooooooh* and *aaaaaah* at the stunning show of lights and colors in the summer sky. If we're close enough, we may be startled by the thunderous popping noises and perhaps catch that unpleasant scent of stale gunpowder. But does anyone complain? Not usually. The whole thing is over in 20 minutes, and that's just part of the experience. It's beautiful and exciting.

On the other hand, if our office building is located right next to the fireworks launch site with daily shows at random times, our attitude is likely to be quite different. The beauty of the fireworks gets lost in the incessant noise, the constant smell of burning, and the distraction of unexpected explosions during our important meetings. We probably wouldn't suggest eliminating all fireworks forever, but we could make a good case for limiting those festive displays to special occasions. For those who are afflicted with *Passion Pistol* syndrome, their enthusiasm can truly be a thing of beauty—but only when it's controlled and applied at the right time. That makes a huge difference in how they are perceived (or misperceived) by the people around them.

Spirited and passionate?

PERCEPTION GAP

Or intense and overzealous?

If you suspect that *Passion Pistol* might be your professional blind spot, ask yourself some important questions. Are you naturally passionate about everything you do or only about certain issues? What things tend to launch you into gunslinger mode? Have you historically been praised for your enthusiasm but now suspect that others aren't always appreciative of your passionate demeanor? Can you pinpoint anything in your past that might trigger your overly enthusiastic response?

The first step in addressing this blind spot is to become more aware of your enthusiasm and its impact on your ability to convey executive presence. Pay close attention to the emotions involved in your interactions with others—your patterns for expressing enthusiasm, the levels of intensity you apply in different situations, and the reactions you get from the people around you. Achieving this type of expanded awareness involves much more than simply *noticing* others' responses. I'm talking about actually tuning in to them on a deeper level so you can determine whether you are being perceived as you intended. Become a more conscious observer of facial expressions, body language and tone. Ask questions to make sure you and your co-workers are on the same page. When you can learn to accurately "read" the people around you, you'll be gathering real-time feedback to help corral your enthusiasm if it gets out of control.

Second, remember that your natural passion isn't like a light switch that should only be turned on or off. Balance is a critical factor. Your enthusiasm has served you well in the past. Take advantage of that! Just temper it with some smart controls and judicious timing. The concept of refining and balancing attributes like enthusiasm to achieve the most successful results is one of the focal points found in my personal branding workbook called *Career Acceleration*. In my opinion, this is a make-it-or-break-it aspect of professional advancement. If you look at the profiles of the world's most admired business executives, you'll find that virtually all of them know how to artfully balance their strengths in a wide range of situations. Just enough power, but not overbearing. Just enough confidence, but not arrogant. Just enough enthusiasm, but not over the top. *You get the idea.*

While working to perfect the skills of walking the enthusiasm tightrope, we all inevitably lose our balance at one point or another. Perhaps a controversial meeting topic prompts a few spur-of-the-moment comments we wish we could take back. Or a quick conversation in the hallway takes a bad turn. It will probably happen, so just be prepared to graciously correct the error after the fact. An apology and a healthy sense of humor can work wonders to alleviate a tense situation. Plus, you'll find that co-workers are more willing to forgive an occasional outburst when it's the exception rather than the rule.

When you can learn to accurately "read" the people around you, you'll be gathering real-time feedback to help corral your enthusiasm if it gets out of control.

Finally, you may find it helpful to re-shape your thinking as it relates to the objectives behind your enthusiasm. Chances are, you have a specific outcome in mind, and you pour every ounce of your passion into making that happen. But is your energetic spirit actually driving away the people who could help you generate the outcome you want? Try taking a less zealous approach in dealing with the key partnerships that can help you achieve your goals. Don't think of it as the need to completely extinguish your naturally vibrant self. Just think "warm spark" instead of "raging inferno."

PERCEPTION 9-1-1

Five Fast Fixes for
Passion Pistol Syndrome

1. Own the weapon. Accept it…you're naturally passionate. That's a good thing! Just use that passion more strategically. Pay attention to how your enthusiasm is perceived in different settings, and use that feedback to adjust your behavior for better results.

2. Scan the horizon. Make it a habit to check the conditions of your work environment. The political climate in a meeting room. Your supervisor's mood. Or the IT department's stress level. Being more aware will help you apply your enthusiasm appropriately and minimize misfires.

3. Aim before firing. If you're quick to send out emotionally charged, rapid-fire messages to anyone in range, you're likely to be perceived as "over the top." Deliberately wait for the right time and gently focus your intensity on the people and issues that matter.

4. Limit your rounds. When you do champion a cause, express yourself using quality rather than quantity. Choose your words carefully. And once you've made your point, head for the holster.

5. Prepare an interpersonal first aid kit. You may not *always* be able to control your hair-trigger emotions. Take notice when your enthusiasm backfires, and be prepared to handle the aftermath. Follow up with colleagues one-on-one and offer a sincere apology if you came on a bit too strong.

Corey's Critical Shift

By the time I was introduced to Corey, the criticism from her performance review had been replaying in her head like a constant loop for nearly two months. Rotating through cycles of frustration, disbelief, resentment and anger, she completely disengaged from everything related to her job. Her new strategy was to fly under the radar, finish her work, and maintain the status quo. She completely silenced her usual roar of enthusiasm, but that tactic wasn't turning out to be very productive for Corey or the company. Even the subordinates who always adored her were not responding well to her obvious apathy. A concerned colleague recognized the drastic change and gave Corey my phone number.

During our first meeting, Corey's aggravation came through loud and clear. She quickly brought me up to speed. According to Corey, it doesn't pay to be fully engaged and passionate about your job. Enthusiasm just results in criticism. Her new reality—post-performance review—was coasting quietly through the workday to avoid any conflict. She tried to sound convincing about this new approach, but I could see that it left her feeling stifled and detached. Sitting on the sidelines went completely against her nature.

I started by asking Corey to make a list of the attributes that were responsible for building her overall career success (ignoring the most recent feedback for the moment). Many of the words on her list had a common thread. *Energy. Enthusiasm. Commitment. Dedication.* Corey clearly saw herself as a producer, a driver of results, and an activist. I reminded her that one negative performance review doesn't cancel out the intrinsic value of her strongest differentiators.

My first challenge was helping Corey truly realize that her passion didn't have to be an all-or-nothing proposition. We talked more about her hands-off stance in the previous eight weeks and its impact on her own performance, the morale of her staff members, and the opinions of her colleagues. Trying to masquerade as someone disengaged and uninvolved was easily causing her more inner turmoil than the painful critique. After an honest assessment, Corey could see that eliminating all traces of her passion could be just as detrimental to her career as letting it run wild. Ultimately, she made a commitment to gaining the benefits of her 500-megawatt enthusiasm rather than simply turning off the lights.

One negative performance review doesn't cancel out the intrinsic value of Corey's strongest differentiators.

To achieve that goal, Corey needed to find the right balance, leveraging the advantages of her natural enthusiasm while managing its impact. I talked with Corey about the specific instances when her passion had propelled her career, as well as times when it derailed her progress. Through that exercise, Corey discovered a distinct trend. When she was under stress or faced with an unexpected obstacle, her quick-fire approach seemed to escalate and develop a much sharper edge. She was also able to identify the hot-button issues that were most likely to fuel an unnecessary surge in enthusiasm. Understanding and anticipating these situations would help her boost awareness during a potentially volatile moment and jump-start the process of keeping her passion under control.

Another area we explored in our coaching sessions together was the unyielding sense of responsibility that Corey felt for the people who reported to her. Perhaps because she never had much support from her own family, she subconsciously vowed to protect and care for her team—her work family—as if her life depended on it. On one hand, her passionate role as advocate and evangelist on behalf of her staff members was commendable. On the other hand, colleagues outside of her immediate group sometimes misinterpreted her animated team spirit as a competitive tactic. In their eyes, Corey's high-energy approach was a potential threat when upper management was doling out the best resources, perks or assignments.

Boosting her awareness during a potentially volatile moment could help Corey jump-start the process of keeping her passion under control.

Once Corey understood the different perceptions that greeted her enthusiasm—and the reasons behind them—she was able to manage her energy level and focus it on people and situations that were more likely to produce the results she wanted. Slowly but surely, she became more skilled at "reading" her colleagues' nonverbal cues and deliberately adjusting her behavior to avoid overwhelming them. She was pleasantly surprised to find that simply tuning in more closely to the people around her was making a big difference in her professional relationships.

As a back-up plan, I helped Corey to develop some strategic recovery techniques to deploy whenever her passion got the best of her. Over time, she learned to disengage during the heat of the moment if she sensed that the best outcome would occur by putting some distance between an event and her response. By acting quickly when she suspected a perception disconnect and handling situations with finesse, she was able to maintain her credibility, reinforce the relationships with her colleagues, and delicately revisit offending subjects. She became quite skilled at offering a sincere apology and communicating her original intent with a calm, collaborative undercurrent. As time went on, she didn't have to implement the back-up plan quite as often, but she was always amazed that her co-workers responded so warmly to this approach.

In my last meeting with Corey, she reported that her efforts to manage and control her boisterous enthusiasm were showing positive results. Wielding her more sophisticated brand of passion, she established stronger networks, improved her performance, and quickly landed on her company's list of rising stars. Today Corey is a highly respected vice president and gracefully leads the top-performing division within her organization.

"Some of us think holding on makes us strong; but sometimes it is letting go."

HERMANN HESSE
(Nobel Prize-Winning Author)

APPLIED SELF-AWARENESS

If your professional blind spot might be *Passion Pistol* syndrome, you may find these action items helpful:

1 Think about the reasons behind your naturally enthusiastic demeanor. Have you always possessed that attribute? If not, when did it seem to emerge? Are there any events or situations that might have heightened this trait? Have you been rewarded for exhibiting highly energetic behavior in the past?

My Action Items: _____

_____

_____

_____

2 Make a list of the times your passionate approach has helped you—and when it hurt you. Any patterns or trends? When and why are you most likely to let your enthusiasm go overboard? Knowing when a potential powder keg is lurking may allow you to eliminate the sparks that could label you as a zealot.

My Action Items: _____

_____

_____

_____

3 Search for balance with your passion. Remind yourself that your enthusiasm is an outstanding, sustainable value you can offer to any employer or client; it simply needs to be controlled and managed to generate positive results.

My Action Items: _____

_____

_____

4 Deliberately raise your level of awareness. Watch for cues that others might be overwhelmed by your enthusiasm or potentially misinterpreting it as a territorial clash.

My Action Items: _____

_____

_____

5 Update or refine the way you express yourself. You can still be a solid advocate for people, projects or ideas without using a high-pressured "hard sell" on every occasion. With your word choice, tone and facial expressions, strive to be perceived as influential rather than forceful—a true sign of executive presence.

My Action Items: _____

_____

_____

_____

6 Pay particular attention to your enthusiasm level during stressful situations. Even when you've mastered the art of balancing your passion and monitoring external feedback, those skills can get lost when critical deadlines are looming and major decisions hang in the balance. Remind yourself to switch into high-alert mode as a precautionary measure.

My Action Items: _____

_____

_____

7 Learn how and when to gracefully let go of an issue you are championing. Even with all of your energy and passion targeted at influencing a particular decision, you won't always be able to control the outcome. Continuing to ramp up your enthusiasm at that point will probably backfire. Instead, you can enhance your reputation by pulling back from an issue while maintaining a collaborate spirit and a positive attitude.

My Action Items: _____

_____

_____

8 Don't panic if your enthusiasm still bubbles over on occasion. Just be prepared with a solid recovery plan, and follow up individually with a humble apology if needed.

My Action Items: _____

_____

CHAPTER 10

Perpetual Doer

A mid-level manager with a prominent energy services company, Leslie never met a To-Do list she didn't like. Few people could match her ability to organize projects, translate the expected deliverables into a distinct set of action items, and then complete each one with expert efficiency. She loved the challenge of conquering a task with complex logistics and a mountain of details. Her attitude? *Bring it on!* Leslie's fearless perspective made her popular among her co-workers, who all seemed to view her multi-tasking mastery with equal parts of astonishment and appreciation. As for her senior managers, they always knew they could count on Leslie to get the job done. She consistently received high praise for generating great results.

Based on that feedback over the years, Leslie got the clear

message that her value was linked directly to her production. She used her tangible outputs as a way to measure her personal success, and she consciously took on projects that would help to spotlight this notable strength. She had a fail-proof system: create the list, complete the tasks, check them off, follow up, prepare for tomorrow. It was a skill that propelled her through business school and continued to be an asset through the early part of her career.

After proving herself as a reliable, action-oriented professional, Leslie felt that she was ready to advance within her organization. She certainly had impressive credentials that demonstrated her accomplishments and her commitment to the company. However, when Leslie started to broadcast her desire to move up to the executive level, she was met with subtle hesitation that soon appeared to be obvious reservations.

Leslie was genuinely bewildered. She was successful, and she had a stack of magnificent performance reviews to prove it. Her track record showed solid evidence of her abilities, her acumen and her accountability. How could she possibly meet resistance on her way to the top? And if there was a problem, why hadn't anyone bothered to tell her? Leslie refused to believe that her career was destined to plateau in middle management after so much hard work, not to mention deliberate efforts to showcase her talents and refine her skills.

Perception Disconnect

While the people in Leslie's office thought she was an excellent manager, they had trouble envisioning her as a leader at a higher level. They could describe at length the many important *things* she had done. But the picture got fuzzy when they tried to view her value in terms of how many *people* she had involved, inspired and led. Leslie was perceived as a doer, not a driver. Somewhere along the way, she had become pigeonholed as the person with the talent for handling the details rather than seeing the big picture. Leslie has a blind spot that I call *Perpetual Doer* syndrome.

The unfortunate irony for Leslie? Despite being perceived as a *Perpetual Doer*, she was actually quite good at working with other people. She was friendly and likeable, with a great sense of humor that quickly put others at ease. She also had real potential for success in tackling challenges from a broader perspective, but she rarely (if ever) found herself in situations that called for looking beyond the minutiae. Leslie had developed a winning reputation as the go-to person for logistical tasks. At first, it was an honor to always be trusted with the nitty-gritty parts of mission-critical projects. But now that she was considered the default solution for everything that required impeccable attention to detail, she was being held back by the perception that she *couldn't* do more. Even if that perception was wrong, it was blocking her progress.

Leslie had become pigeonholed as the person with the talent for handling the details rather than seeing the big picture.

---

*Perpetual Doer*s are often quite surprised when they discover that their promising careers are suddenly stalled instead of speeding along in the fast lane. It's a shock for them and, on the surface, unexplainable. For the upper-level executives who are forced to provide that explanation and push back against the hopeful *Perpetual Doers*, it's hard to make a case against their achievements and sheer tenacity. These talented employees have frequently done everything asked of them, and they've done it well. By every measure, they have been quite successful. And yet, they just don't seem to be good candidates for leadership at the next level. *Something is missing.*

In the corporate world, that missing ingredient is often referred to as *executive presence*. Most people recognize it when they see it, but quantifying it is almost impossible. People with executive presence are perceived as confident, influential and calmly yet firmly in charge. They can command attention in a room without saying a word, and they know how to accurately "read" the world around them (from political cues to their colleagues' emotions). They actively search for the inevitable blind spots and perception gaps that could potentially damage their reputations—and they correct them. Essentially, these people possess "the business X factor."

If you only remember one thing after reading this book, here's the top take-away: the somewhat-elusive skills collectively described as "executive presence" frequently represent *the only difference* between an outstanding professional who gets marooned in middle management and one who seems to effortlessly rise in the corporate power structure. People with executive presence are masterful when it comes to identifying and eliminating professional blind spots. All other things being equal, the intangible qualities of emotional intelligence and interpersonal skills give these leaders a very tangible edge. And when employees are perceived as having executive presence, they can parlay that positive reputation into faster advancement and a more lucrative career.

Should you have any doubts about the existence of these intangible attributes or the sheer power of their impact, Leslie could quickly convince you that they are real. She discovered that all of her efforts to carve out such a strong identity as an organized manager had inadvertently undermined her own ability to be seen as a true leader, as someone with that coveted X factor. She had all of the potential needed to move to the next level, but she had a *perception problem.* Her colleagues and co-workers didn't see her as a leader with executive presence. If Leslie ever wanted to be seriously considered for advancement, she'd have to change her reputation from a *Perpetual Doer* into a purposeful driver.

Remarkably reliable and high performing?

PERCEPTION GAP

Or one-dimensional and over-functioning?

Though it might seem unfair, we all have a tendency to categorize our co-workers as doers or drivers. Not everyone can be seen as both. Most people begin their careers as doers by the very nature of entry-level positions. At some point, those with the greatest potential make the gradual shift from doing all of the work themselves to making sure that all of the work gets done well. Instead of simply managing, they step up and start leading – delegating, motivating, strategizing. They expand the context of their reputations from doers to drivers by incorporating the subtle yet highly compelling characteristics of executive presence. *Perpetual Doers* struggle to make that transition, and this has a negative impact on the way others view their capacity to advance and handle more sophisticated leadership opportunities.

An open conversation with a supervisor
is an excellent first step toward expanding
your professional focus.

If you think you might be perceived as a *Perpetual Doer*, consider how your co-workers view your workplace contributions. Are you known for a particular skill or talent that is primarily production-oriented? Do others repeatedly seek out your help in that one particular area? Do you volunteer for similar projects because you feel most comfortable with them? Do you sometimes avoid other types of assignments that are less quantifiable and might take you off task? Is it possible that you have created the impression that you're more valuable as a manager/producer rather than a leader/visionary? From an outsider's perspective, does your career look a bit one-dimensional? Have you been pigeonholed in a certain area and now feel as though you are in a professional rut?

Fortunately, there are things you can do to make that critical shift from doer to driver. Start by sharing your goals with the people who have the power to help you make some changes. A sincere and candid discussion with your boss or team leaders could begin to pave the way for taking on different types of projects. Communicate tactfully, be clear about your objectives, and enlist their support with professional development. Many times, an open conversation with a supervisor is an excellent first step toward expanding your professional focus.

Take charge of your own professional development. If your company has opportunities for leadership training, by all means, participate. But even if you do have access to more formal education programs, dive into your own self-paced learning as soon as possible. It's *your* job to understand what's required at the next level and do whatever is necessary to be seen as someone who is ready to progress. Read books on innovation, leadership and strategic thinking. Take classes. Attend workshops or webinars. Investing your time to learn more is a clear signal to upper management that you are serious about getting ahead. Besides, no one else has a greater incentive to make sure you are well prepared for advancement.

Another way to kick-start your campaign for career progress is to find a champion or sponsor within your company who is willing to help promote you throughout higher levels of the organization. This will likely be someone who knows you fairly well, likes you, admires your work, and has first-hand experience with your previous successes. It's also important for this person to be in a secure position within the company and viewed by others as a credible source. Yes, that's a tall order. If someone who fits that description doesn't immediately come to mind, start to beef up your office networking. Whether you uncover the perfect champion or not, you'll find that connecting with colleagues on a deeper level and maintaining these supportive relationships are absolute necessities for careers on the move.

> Investing your time to learn more is a clear signal to upper management that you are serious about getting ahead.

To leverage this concept on a larger scale, you can obtain assistance from several colleague-champions by establishing your own "personal advisory board." Each individual on the board can make a unique contribution to your career success, and you'll have options for support without overburdening any single person. To assemble an effective advisory board for your career, identify potential advisors—successful professionals you genuinely trust—and approach them with the idea of giving you candid feedback about your intended direction. Receiving guidance from a diverse set of people will bring a richer perspective to your career development.

In your current position, start adjusting your approach to getting things done. To put it another way: *delegate more.* It's important to remember that leaders don't do all of the work themselves. They understand their subordinates' strengths and aspirations, and they use that knowledge to effectively match people to tasks in a way that will get optimal results. Make that your new M.O. Be clear about the objectives when giving assignments, but don't allow your perfectionist tendencies to derail the delegation process. If you're not satisfied with the finished product, resist the urge to do it over yourself. Instead, return the work to the person who produced it and make sure that he or she understands your expectations. Using this approach, you are helping your team members increase their own levels of competency while protecting yourself from becoming overburdened.

As your confidence grows, begin taking on projects that will help you gain more leadership experience and exposure, even when they are out of your comfort zone. Working in a different capacity takes courage, but don't be afraid to take risks. This is a key activity in changing the perceptions that are holding you back. If you can't find the right opportunities within your company, look outside of the workplace. Get involved with a professional organization and serve on the Board. Volunteer to speak at an industry event. Demonstrate your thought leadership by submitting an article to a trade publication. The more you stretch and succeed, the more confident and empowered you'll feel. Perhaps more importantly, your supervisors will witness the transformation and begin to reevaluate your potential.

Connecting with colleagues on a deeper level and maintaining these supportive relationships are absolute necessities for careers on the move.

Just like corporations sometimes embark on a rebranding process to take advantage of new profit opportunities, you can do the same thing by updating your own value proposition. Being able to articulate your value in a way that helps others clearly see the benefits of working with you is an essential skill at any level of any organization. I'm not talking about a canned elevator speech or a sentence from the top of your resume. Instead, I'm referring to the stories and examples you weave into conversations to demonstrate your unique contributions to corporate success. As you make the transition away from the *Perpetual Doer*, be sure to update the stories you tell so you are communicating your abilities to lead at a higher level. To change perceptions, you need to change the way you are defined. Sharing your value proposition gives you a casual yet extremely powerful way to prove that you aren't a one-trick pony.

Finally, work on developing your own version of executive presence. Study the senior leaders who seem to possess those professional X-factor characteristics, and try to emulate their behaviors. Take authorship of your ideas, and present them in a decisive and convincing manner. Resist the urge to qualify your statements or make apologies. Manage your emotions when you make requests or set limits. Remember that the cumulative effect of your verbal, nonverbal and visual cues will determine the messages received by your colleagues and the perceptions they form about your abilities and potential.

The somewhat-elusive skills collectively described as "executive presence" frequently represent *the only difference* between an outstanding professional who gets marooned in middle management and one who seems to effortlessly rise in the corporate power structure.

PERCEPTION 9-1-1

Five Fast Fixes for
Perpetual Doer Syndrome

1. **Speak up.** Talk to your supervisor more specifically about your career goals, and discuss concrete options to help you achieve them. A gentle approach and appropriate timing are critical, but you know what they say about the squeaky wheel…

2. **Be prepared.** Breaking out of the mold to reach next-level leadership likely requires some different skills. To make sure you are ready when the opportunities come along, prepare to move out of your comfort zone. Take on stretch assignments. Teach a course. Work closely with a mentor or leadership coach you trust.

3. **Shift your focus.** Make the conscious effort to adjust the way you think about your daily tasks. Shift from the tactical to the strategic. Look beyond the details to the people. Put the emphasis on leading rather than managing.

4. **Climb into the driver's seat.** Start delegating, and actively seek out projects that will allow you to show off your leadership skills. Both are visible ways to begin changing the false perception that you can't take the wheel.

5. **Redefine your value.** You are your own best salesperson, so make sure you are presenting the features and benefits that position you as a perfect choice for *senior leadership*. Update your value proposition, and weave in new examples. By painting a new picture of the value you offer, others will start to see you in a new light.

Key Lessons for Leslie

When Leslie confided in a colleague about feeling sabotaged by her own hard work, the woman passed along my name and phone number. Leslie arrived at our first meeting with a large folder containing a wide range of documents to substantiate her success. As she began to describe her achievements, page by page, I could instantly tell that her career roadblock wasn't caused by a missing page in her impressive file. *Perpetual Doer* syndrome was an easy diagnosis.

First, I wanted to help relieve some of Leslie's anxiety about feeling trapped in the middle-management cage. She had already mastered the essentials, and she had done so many things right. (Just check out that folder!) She was truly on the verge of getting ahead. The changes she needed to make were relatively small and, oddly enough, mostly related to adjusting her perception among her colleagues. She had the brains, the drive and the determination to accelerate her career; she just needed to change her reputation to be seen as someone who could lead people and craft strategies. I assured her that she had the potential to continue her upward career trajectory. Although I saw a glimpse of hopefulness in her eyes, I could tell she wasn't quite convinced.

My first challenge for Leslie was to begin delegating more projects to her own staff members. On a logical level, that made perfect sense to her. However, Leslie confessed that the thought of "delegating more and doing less" seemed just plain wrong. I asked her to start thinking about that in a fresh way. The hours she gained through delegation shouldn't be viewed as wasted, non-productive downtime. On the contrary. Loosening up her schedule would give Leslie a chance to think about the bigger picture and formulate smarter plans for better results. While she didn't have much experience working from that perspective, it was exactly what she needed to stretch in a new direction. She agreed to give it a shot.

Given Leslie's strong slant toward productivity, I knew she would feel more in control of the situation if we started by creating an action plan for professional development. I asked Leslie to make a list of the knowledge and skills she thought she would need as a senior leader within her organization. Among her responses: thinking strategically, influencing teams, and coming up with innovative ideas. Based on that list, we crafted a blueprint for her development process, complete with courses to take, books to read, and workshops to attend. We also brainstormed about opportunities to showcase her leadership talents in a more visible, perception-changing way. I encouraged her to begin attending monthly Leadership Luncheons held in her area, and she also planned to volunteer as a facilitator for a regional conference with a national trade organization. These were all tasks she could work on right away, which instantly helped to begin alleviating her frustration.

Next, I asked Leslie to tell me about some of the leaders she most admired within her company and describe their behaviors, attitudes and approaches. At first, Leslie focused on their functional abilities for things like public speaking or deciphering complex market trends. I pushed her to look beyond those things and find the less-obvious attributes that set them apart from their peers. How did they interact with other people at all levels? What kind of word choices, tone and body language did they employ? How did they influence and inspire teams to reach their goals? I could tell that Leslie was beginning to recognize the subtle nuances that separated the rising stars from all the rest. Degrees didn't matter. Titles didn't matter. Years of experience didn't matter. What *did* matter was their emotional intelligence, their mastery of these intangible skills. In other words, the primary differentiator for the top leaders was their executive presence.

Leslie's response echoed so many others I have heard in my years of coaching. *"Ok, I get it. I see it. But I don't know how to do it."* Of course, trying to precisely define executive presence is about as easy as trying to cure the common cold. Luckily, there were things that Leslie could do to increase her intangible leadership skills. Once she learned to integrate some of these powerful traits and visibly demonstrate her readiness to advance, I was certain that Leslie's colleagues would begin to perceive her as authentic executive material.

For Leslie to get noticed and get ahead, she needed to look the part of a promotable executive. Like it or not, her credibility was often based on her visual resume. While Leslie routinely wore professional attire, we talked about the subtle messages she might be sending with her dress and her grooming. By stepping up her image just a notch to more closely match her company's top executives, she could make a bolder statement about her potential that would support her new leadership skills and behaviors.

I also asked Leslie to become more aware of her patterns of communication. She could benefit by watching and imitating the distinct interaction styles of many successful senior executives. Specifically, they tend to be excellent listeners. When they do speak, they use succinct language based on well-organized thoughts, controlled and purposeful timing, and powerful pauses.

Using some role-play exercises, Leslie was able to experiment with integrating these techniques into her own conversational style. She caught on quickly, and I noticed her progress as we talked in subsequent meetings.

Leslie was beginning to recognize the subtle nuances
that separated the rising stars from all the rest.
The primary differentiator for the top leaders was
their executive presence.

We also discussed the role of nonverbal communications in the profile of leaders with executive presence. Leslie honed in on their deliberate use of gestures and their ability to make their voices land with impact. She recognized their upright stance, relaxed yet energetic posture, and steady eye contact. Leslie also saw the importance of minimizing her nervous hand gestures and fidgeting, which would detract from the image she hoped to project. All of these revelations gave Leslie clear direction on ways to interact with more of that "executive feeling."

Positioning herself as a thought leader was another way that Leslie could establish herself as a strong candidate for advancement. Thought leaders develop an area of expertise that is valuable to their companies, and they actively apply their knowledge in a way that results in a unique understanding or a distinct opinion about that topic. They can spot trends and see implications in this area much more clearly than their counterparts. In that specific niche, thought leaders have moved from *informed* to *influential*. I challenged Leslie to follow her passion and work toward becoming perceived as an expert in some area of her industry. Developing and expressing her point of view as a thought leader would give her company a competitive advantage and expand her professional reputation as a strategic, visionary thinker.

While these steps would help Leslie look and sound more like a leader, I wanted to make sure that she also understood the critical role of social fluency. To be perceived as someone with executive presence, she needed to operate at all times with a higher level of emotional intelligence. We talked about connecting with colleagues on a deeper level and learning to read (even anticipate) the emotions and reactions of others. This skill requires more practice and continuous application, but Leslie recognized its importance. Just by being more aware of social cues and their implications, she was ahead of the curve.

Developing and expressing her point of view as a thought leader would give her company a competitive advantage and expand Leslie's professional reputation as a strategic, visionary thinker.

At one point in our meetings, Leslie mentioned her conversations with a senior vice president at the company. When I asked her more about this woman, she told me that they had met at a corporate event several years ago and developed a positive working relationship. I suggested that she approach this woman about being her mentor and helping to guide her through the process of enhancing her professional reputation.

As I suspected, this woman was extremely receptive to the idea and happily accepted. She provided Leslie with valuable feedback on her perceived performance and also kept Leslie's name in the mix for new projects and possible promotions. Nurturing this relationship ended up being an enormous asset to Leslie as she worked to accelerate her career.

Leslie's confidence grew quickly, and her leadership persona was starting to get some real traction. She was taking on more projects that showed off her new skills and was beginning to get recognition for a different type of success. About a year after our last meeting, Leslie called to share some good news. She had recently been selected for a senior director position, and she was beyond thrilled with her new responsibilities. She had genuinely learned to "let go" of the details more than she ever thought possible, and she was embracing her new reputation as a visionary leader. Even through the phone, I recognized the clear signs of executive presence in her voice and demeanor. Leslie had successfully crossed the bridge from doer to driver, and I could tell that she loved the view from the other side.

*"Hunker down in your comfort zone,
and the world will pass you by."*

DENNIS E. COATES, PH.D.
(Leadership Expert & Author)

APPLIED SELF-AWARENESS

If your professional blind spot might be *Perpetual Doer* syndrome, these action items may be helpful as you begin the process of making positive changes:

1 Determine whether your current reputation is holding your career hostage. How do your colleagues perceive your capacity to lead? Are you seen as a doer rather than a driver? How could you benefit by stretching and expanding that perception?

My Action Items: _____

_____

_____

_____

2 Communicate openly with your boss about your desire to advance. Be assertive in asking for new opportunities. If your supervisors know your intentions, they will likely be willing to help you take the next steps.

My Action Items: _____

_____

_____

_____

_____

3 Understand the expectations of moving to the next level, and make sure you are prepared to get there. Professional development is up to you, so pursue the learning opportunities that will help you gain the knowledge and skills you will need to advance.

My Action Items: _____

_____

_____

4 Get comfortable with delegating tasks to your team members. Remember that your value won't be measured purely on production, so you can earn more respect by displaying your ability to think, lead and inspire.

My Action Items: _____

_____

_____

5 Set boundaries to avoid taking on the same kinds of projects that have pigeonholed you in the past. Request assignments that will help you gain a different set of skills. Being visible as you work in a new capacity will help to add depth and dimension to your reputation.

My Action Items: _____

_____

_____

_____

6 Look for additional opportunities to boost your skills outside of the corporate environment. You may be able to stretch toward a leadership position at work because of the experiences you gain while volunteering with a professional organization or a community group. And never underestimate the power of networking.

My Action Items: _____

_____

_____

7 Dress, act and speak as though you are already at the management level you hope to attain. Increase your self-awareness, as well as your social fluency. These smart adjustments can make a huge difference in helping to change perceptions about your capacity for leadership at a higher level.

My Action Items: _____

_____

_____

8 Get the support of a mentor, a champion or even a personal advisory board. People you trust and admire can give you honest feedback regarding your progress and help to ensure that you are considered for new opportunities and promotions.

My Action Items: _____

_____

_____

9 Refocus your leadership brand. How do you describe what you do to others? What stories or examples do you share to demonstrate your expertise? Don't let those responses run on automatic pilot. Update your value proposition to incorporate your leadership skills and your more ambitious goals for advancement. Strive to position yourself as a thought leader, and speak up to make sure that others understand the new scope of your capabilities.

My Action Items: _____

_____

_____

_____

_____

10 Take steps to incorporate the elusive elements of executive presence into your own professional identity. Keep an eye on the people within your organization who exhibit these traits, and learn from their examples.

My Action Items: _____

_____

_____

_____

_____

CHAPTER 11

Your Personal Blind Spots

Throughout this book, we've looked at the classic blind spots that seem to be most common in derailing careers and preventing even the most brilliant people from reaching their full potential. Virtually everyone can quickly think of a co-worker who matches some of the profiles described. (They are called "blind spots" for a great reason: they're always easier to pinpoint in *other people*.) Perhaps you even identified closely with one of the case studies. Based on my experiences from years of coaching, I can tell you that it is quite common for people to see glimpses of themselves in many of the blind-spot stories. Even those who don't readily relate to a certain gap can often think of a particular situation where a brief lapse in awareness produced the same symptoms. It happens to the best of us.

Additional Perception Gaps

We are all susceptible to perception disconnects, and there are dozens (if not hundreds) of blind spots with the potential to tarnish our reputations. The resulting gaps that impact our reputations can occur with many different variations, each of them potentially layered and interconnected. Here are a few additional examples that may sound familiar or remind you of other colleagues you've encountered:

People who feel they are:	But others perceive them as:
Colorful; dramatic; bold	Attention-seeking; disruptive; poor listeners; rebellious; over-the-top
Meticulous; diligent; detail-oriented	Nit-picky; boring; micromanagers
Dutiful; loyal; accommodating	Reluctant to act independently; easily swayed by popular opinion; lacking in confidence
Decisive; quick to think on their feet; strong leaders	Inflexible; uninterested in others' thoughts and ideas; volatile
Careful; thorough; practical	Overly conservative; skeptical; highly risk-averse
Reserved; quiet; shy	Indifferent; uncommunicative; unfriendly; aloof

My intention for telling you that perception gaps are surprisingly plentiful is not to spread doom and gloom. Just the opposite, in fact. After reading this book, you have gained some insight to help you recognize and correct professional blind spots—whatever they are, however they are blended, and whenever they show up. The action plans that conclude each chapter can guide you in closing a certain gap or simply boosting your overall emotional intelligence. Either way, you'll be better prepared by simply knowing about the potential pitfalls in advance and, hopefully, avoiding some of them. Understanding the concepts of self-awareness and perception gaps will give you a clear edge in preventing these intangible career barricades from impeding your forward progress.

Strategies to Find and Fix Your Blind Spots

For those of you who want a more specific roadmap, I do want to leave you with some tools to help you pinpoint and correct your own personal blind spots. The four steps that follow should prove to be quite valuable:

1. Increase your self-awareness.

Before you can determine whether other people are defining your professional reputation exactly in the manner you'd prefer, you'll want to fully understand your own goals and intentions. How would you like to be perceived? What is your *ideal* reputation? To find those answers, you'll need to increase your own self-awareness. Set aside some time to seriously consider the following questions and jot down your thoughts for reference:

- What are your strongest and most developed skills?
- How do people benefit from working with you?
- What are the results of your communications and interactions with others?
- How do you make others feel?

- How would you ideally like to be described by the people who work with you?
- Is your ideal reputation realistic and attainable?
- How could that reputation impact your opportunities for advancement?

2. Seek out candid feedback.

Regardless of your goals and ideals, what is your *actual* reputation in the workplace? Uncomfortable or not, we need to know how we're perceived. And that means we need to ask! While this conclusion might seem obvious, many people think that making an educated guess is good enough. Not true. To get an accurate picture of our blind spots, we must gather actual feedback from those who have real experience interacting with us. Ideally, you'll want to get input from people who have observed your behaviors and communication styles for a minimum of six months.

- Managers, directors, supervisors and bosses
  (*current and former*)
- Peers, co-workers and colleagues
  (*across departments and teams*)
- Staff, subordinates and employees
- Members of common committees or organizations
  (*professional or civic/community*)
- Advisors and friends from college
- Family members

When making a list of people to approach, consider these thoughts. Choose those you respect and feel confident would have your best interests in mind. Comments from a colleague who is competing for the same promotion or bonus might be a bit suspect. Make sure you select people you trust to give you candid and specific information. A glowing review with exclusively positive remarks might warm your heart, but it won't help you get an accurate picture of any perception gaps that are lurking. Sometimes the best people to approach are ones with whom you have experienced some difficulties in the past. They are likely to shed light on a few issues you find hard to see—which is precisely the goal of this exercise. Not necessarily pleasant, but extremely valuable in making changes with real impact.

Once we figure out which people to approach, we need to determine how to start the process. As you'll see, we have plenty of options for gathering feedback and evaluating our reputations.

- Official 360° assessments and evaluations
  (*available from many Leadership and
  Industrial/Organizational Psychology Institutes*)
- Self-designed questionnaires distributed in person or online with sites like Survey Monkey
- Formal performance reviews from supervisors
- Candid conversations with mentors or advisors
- Informal dialog with trusted colleagues
- Casual comments from co-workers
  (*sometimes disguised as humor*)

As an alternative, I invite you to visit my website at www.SaraCanaday.com for more information about my *Career Acceleration* workbook. This self-paced guide includes a concise, ready-to-use feedback survey you might find helpful, as well as a unique method for quantifying and even graphing your perception gaps in 12 distinct categories. *(See Figure 2 on Page 172 for an example.)*

FIGURE 2

Perception Attributes

How would you like to be described by your colleagues and co-workers? How would they actually describe you? What's the difference?

Action-Oriented	Dramatic	Open-Minded
Adaptable	Driven	Optimistic
Aloof	Dynamic	Organized
Approachable	Empathetic	Passionate
Articulate	Energetic	Persuasive
Assertive	Engaging	Precise
Authoritative	Ethical	Predictable
Big (Personality)	Executive	Quirky
Calm	Extroverted	Relatable
Carefree	Focused	Risk-Taking
Caring	Formal	Scattered
Casual	Forward-Thinking	Self-Conscious
Cautious	Friendly	Sensitive
Collaborative	Genuine	Shy
Comfortable	Global	Sophisticated
Commanding	Good Listener	Spontaneous
Competitive	Humble	Strategic Driver
Composed	Humorous	Successful
Conceptual	Impatient	Supportive
Confident	Industrious	Trusting
Connected	Inspiring	Unpredictable
Conservative	Intense	Visionary
Convincing	International	Other:
Creative	Introverted	
Credible	Insensitive	_____
Decisive	Leader-Like	_____
Dependable	Likeable	
Detached	Methodical	_____
Diplomatic	Mysterious	_____

*Excerpts from **Career Acceleration: Speed Up Your Success With Strategic Personal Branding** by Sara Canaday. © 2011. Workbooks available for purchase at www.SaraCanaday.com.*

Perception Ratings

How would you rate yourself on the following scales? What ratings would you receive from colleagues and co-workers? How would the average scores differ?

		LOW				AVERAGE					HIGH
1.	**Self-Awareness** *(aware of own strengths, weaknesses and emotions, and how those impact decisions and behaviors)*	1	2	3	4	5	6	7	8	9	10
2.	**Decision-Making Skills** *(ability to solve problems and think independently)*	1	2	3	4	5	6	7	8	9	10
3.	**Stress Tolerance** *(ability to maintain composure despite adversity)*	1	2	3	4	5	6	7	8	9	10
4.	**Adaptability** *(flexibility and agility; willingness to change course)*	1	2	3	4	5	6	7	8	9	10
5.	**Attention to Dress & Grooming**	1	2	3	4	5	6	7	8	9	10
6.	**Effective Use of Body Language**	1	2	3	4	5	6	7	8	9	10
7.	**Mood & Demeanor**	1	2	3	4	5	6	7	8	9	10
8.	**Energy Level**	1	2	3	4	5	6	7	8	9	10
9.	**Interpersonal Skills** *(ability to communicate and listen effectively)*	1	2	3	4	5	6	7	8	9	10
10.	**Approachability & Capacity to Build Rapport**	1	2	3	4	5	6	7	8	9	10
11.	**Empathy** *(ability to recognize and understand others' perspectives)*	1	2	3	4	5	6	7	8	9	10
12.	**Collaboration** *(ability to work successfully as part of a team)*	1	2	3	4	5	6	7	8	9	10
		LOW				AVERAGE					HIGH

However you decide to gather your feedback, just do it. And if the prospect of measuring your reputation prompts you to immediately brace yourself and assume the crash position, you might be pleasantly surprised. Gathering feedback isn't exclusively about identifying your shortcomings. You may very well uncover some hidden strengths you never recognized but your colleagues have noticed and appreciated. Whether the comments you collect are positive or negative, push yourself to think of them as a tool for your professional development. By positioning your feedback as a valuable asset rather than a judgment or criticism, you'll be able to analyze it objectively and apply it in a much more productive manner.

3. Close the gaps.

Once you've gathered honest feedback, you'll have what you need to answer the big question: what's the difference between what you intend (your ideal reputation) and what they perceive (your actual reputation)? **If the intentions and perceptions don't match, you've uncovered a blind spot.** Sometimes the newly found blind spot doesn't really impact your career, and you can simply file the information away in your brain for future reference. In other instances though, you've discovered a clear opportunity for improvement by closing the perception gaps. The action plans and suggestions throughout this book are an excellent starting point for making those changes. Still, human behavior is not an exact science. There is no algorithm that produces a definitive solution for Blind Spot #27. Unique situations and diverse personalities make that impossible. On the upside, you are now armed with the most important weapon possible in the battle to close your perception gaps: *applied self-awareness.*

Pay attention to behavior (yours and theirs). Then turn your insight into action for positive impact. It's not a mathematical equation, but it does sum up the process in its simplest form.

As you work toward your goals, be sure to keep in mind the critical role of balance. Think of the gap-closing process as fine-tuning rather than full-tilt, shoot-for-the-other-end-of-the-spectrum change. For example, the reserved and introspective guy in the office who discovers that his colleagues perceive him as disengaged doesn't need to wash down his bacon and eggs every morning with a Red Bull. The result might not be, *"Isn't Jim's new energy level impressive?"* but rather, *"Is Jim on drugs or what?"* Overcorrecting frequently creates a new and different problem. He would be wise to slowly adjust his messages and behaviors in search of that "sweet spot" range, the place where his intentions match up with his co-workers' perceptions and align with his own natural tendencies. Sometimes minor adjustments can have a major impact, so try to use a carefully balanced approach as you work to close your perception gaps.

4. Be prepared for change.

Our business environment today is in a constant state of change—the economy, the needs of our customers, the products and services our companies offer, the competition, the technology we employ, the members of our teams. Coping with the challenges of perpetual change is a necessary part of becoming successful within any organization. But it also has two important implications in terms of managing the perceptions that shape our reputations and our careers.

First, you can gain a real edge by gathering perception feedback on an ongoing basis, making it a natural and automatic component of your interactions with others. You can't assume that the attributes you've worked so hard to nudge into that "sweet spot" range will still be optimal six months from now or when you're suddenly working with a new global team. Change happens. Keep checking for new blind spots! If you can integrate feedback collection (verbal or nonverbal) into all of your conversations with other people, you'll have the benefit of instant, real-time results as a priceless guide to your next move. Periodically, you'll still want to repeat a more formal feedback analysis, but consciously reading the reactions of people around you (and even learning to anticipate those reactions) will help you make the simple adjustments that can noticeably set you apart from your peers.

Second, your knowledge of perceptions can prepare you to maneuver through the new challenges and changing expectations that come with professional advancement. Few people discuss it, but those who move to the top of an organization are subjected to an unwritten yet very real shift in expectations. When trying to close their reputation-perception gaps, senior-level managers face a task that can be much more complex. Why? To be successful, great leaders need the capacity to exhibit complementary (or even opposite) attributes in certain situations: confident yet humble, visionary yet realistic, strategic yet creative, competitive yet empathetic, energetic yet calm in a crisis, decisive yet flexible, strong yet able to show vulnerability. The basic, straightforward behaviors that allowed them to get ahead early on in their careers suddenly don't fit with the executive persona.

The rising corporate stars who fail to grasp the changing requirements and this seemingly paradoxical set of new expectations end up with high levels of frustration and stalled careers. You, on the other hand, already know the benefits of using feedback regularly, managing the perceptions of others, and maintaining a positive reputation. If you can master these skills, you'll have a solid advantage when navigating the upper echelons of the corporate world.

CHAPTER 12

Final Thoughts

Whether we like it or not, perception is reality. Having the best of intentions isn't enough to get us the new job, the big raise or the highly coveted promotion. Our professional reputations are defined through the perceptual lens of our colleagues, co-workers and clients—and those reputations determine the path and the pace of our careers (for better or worse).

The truth is, we *all* have blind spots in some area. No one is so amazingly self-aware that he or she can clearly see and eliminate every potential perception disconnect before it occurs. Those who are most successful have just learned how to read the diverse people and situations they encounter and respond appropriately. Sure, they are savvy enough to avoid the obvious perception landmines. But they have also mastered a skill that could be even more important: recognizing an inadvertent "hit" and diving in quickly for effective damage control. *Insight to action.*

The world's strongest leaders today know how to manage the perception gaps that are inevitable in our fast-paced, technology-fueled, global business environment. That's why *You — According to Them* isn't simply a book title. It's a mindset that captures the importance of actively working to understand our reputations and artfully managing the perceptions that directly impact our careers. I hope you'll be able to apply this concept long after you've read the final page of the book, and I sincerely hope it gives you a competitive advantage with unparalleled success.

 A rare blend of analytical entrepreneur and perceptive warmth, **Sara Canaday** has a unique gift for helping high-potential professionals to achieve their best. Sara began her journey working full-time while she earned an MBA. As she climbed the ladder of corporate America, she repeatedly observed a surprising phenomenon: the most successful people weren't necessarily the ones with the highest IQs or best job skills. She recognized instead that career advancement was much more closely linked with *how* people applied their knowledge and talents—their capacity to collaborate, communicate, and influence others.

Because of this revelation early on, Sara developed an uncanny ability to pinpoint the sometimes-unlikely yet pivotal attributes that could make or break a career, and she was able to convey that information in a compassionately candid way. Colleagues, subordinates and superiors alike frequently approached Sara for her advice on overcoming career hurdles and developing strategies to increase their personal market value. Despite reaching an executive position in operations with a major company, Sara realized that helping others to maximize their career potential was truly her life's work.

Today, Sara is happily fulfilling that commitment as a speaker, consultant, coach, author and owner of her rapidly growing firm, Sara Canaday & Associates. This venue has given her the opportunity to mentor and support thousands of people in diverse situations, inspiring many of them to move from insight to action with dramatic career results.

Sara lives in Austin, Texas, with her husband Brandon, her daughter Taylor, and her son Cole. She proudly follows the same advice she shares with her clients: be honest with yourself, never stop finding ways to improve, and—*if all else fails*—head to Starbucks for a Double Mocha Latte with extra whipped cream.

For more information or to purchase Sara's nationally acclaimed **Career Acceleration** *workbook on strategic personal branding, please visit* **www.SaraCanaday.com***. You can also sign up to receive Sara's e-newsletter, packed with valuable information and resources to support your career success.*

INDEX

Abrupt, 46–49
Academic achievement. *See* Credentials
Accommodating, 168
Action-oriented, 65–67, 146–50
Active listening, 41, 60, 118, 128
Adaptability, 173. *See also* Change; *Frozen Compass*
Adversarial, 97–102
After-hours events, 17, 86
All-or-nothing thinking, 87–88, 98–102
Aloof, 80–85, 168
Amiable. *See* Personable
Angelou, Maya (quoted), 122
Apathy, 138–41
Apologetic tendency, 62
Apologizing, 137, 141
Applied self-awareness, 7–8, 174–75
Art of influence, 101–2, 108. *See also* Thought leader
Assertive, 111–14. *See also* Directness
Assessment. *See* Self-assessment
Assumptions about direct communication, 61
Attention-seeking, 168
Authority. *See also* Resistance to Authority
 basing it only on intellect, 31–32
 becoming an accepted, 104–5
 wearing it with conviction, 62
Awareness of others, 77, 135, 137, 143. *See also* Self-awareness

Balancing
 costs and benefits, 105
 displays of emotion, 85, 93
 enthusiasm and timing, 135–36, 143
 productive with personal, 53–54
 pros and cons of new ideas, 106
 when changing your approach, 175
Bar-On EQ-i® assessment, 87
Battles, picking your, 100
Beliefs. *See* Limiting Beliefs
Big picture, importance of sharing, 54
Black-and-white thinking, 87–88, 98–102
Bland, 111–14
Blind spots. *See also* Perception gaps
 about, 167
 benefits of illuminating one's, 6–7

Confidence, 36. *See also* Lacking confidence
Controlled, feeling. *See Don't Fence Me In*
Convincing, 154
Coolness under pressure, 87
Cooperative tone of voice, 26
Corey (case study), 131–32, 138–41. *See also Passion Pistol*
Corporate policies. *See* Rules of the workplace
Cost-benefit analysis, 101, 103, 107
Courage, 126
Co-workers. *See also* Art of influence; Resentment
    acknowledging talents of, 36, 70
    adjusting personal interactions with, 46–51, 71
    alerting, about changes to your style, 53
    compromising with, 101–2
    doers vs. drivers, 149–54
    protective stance toward, 131–32
    showing interest in, 84–85, 93
    soliciting discussion from, 50
    tuning into cues from, 137, 140–41
    using sales techniques with, 22–24
Creative thinking, 16, 101
Credentials. *See also* Intangible skill sets
    alone, not enough, 112, 124
    and success in business, 2–3, 29–31
Criticism, dealing with, 138–41

Deadline-setting, 71, 73
Decision-making skills, 173
Decisive, 46–49, 62, 168
Dedicated, 138–41
Delegating work, 152–53, 156–57, 163
Dependable. *See* Perpetual Doer
Detached. *See* Indifferent
Detail-oriented, 147, 168
Devil's advocate, 104–5, 107
Diligent, 168
Diploma. *See* Credentials
Diplomatic, 128
Directness. *See also* Assertive; Not direct enough; Too direct
    how to adjust the level, 53–63
    why adjust the level, 48–52
Disagreeing with others, 20
Disconnects. *See* Perception gaps
Disruptive, 168
Distant, 88–90
Doer. *See Perpetual Doer*
Dominance, 40
Don't Fence Me In. See also Clint (case study)
    applied self-awareness, 25–28
    five fast fixes, 20
    perception gap, 15–19
Dramatic, 168
Dress and grooming, 158–61, 165
Driven, 67–70

Practical, 97–102, 168
Precise, 95–97
Pressure. *See also* Pace of work
    on staff, 72–74
    staying cool under, 87
Private knowledge, 9f–10
Problem-solving skills, 103
Productivity. *See also* Highly productive
    measuring your success by, 145–46
    problem for staff, 65–67, 72–75
    relation to directness, 49–50
    ways to maximize, 58
Professional advancement. *See also* Executive presence
    importance of reputation to, 4
    self-employment as part of, 28
    skills needed for, 34–35
Professional development, 151, 157. *See also* Learning on the job
    getting feedback as part of, 174
    pursuing outside of work, 165
Public knowledge, 9f–10

Quick-thinking, 168
Quiet, 168

Rational leader, 47
Realistic, 97–102. *See also* Unrealistic
Rebellious, 15–19, 168
Rebranding yourself, 153–54, 165. *See also* Reputation (your own);
        Value proposition
Reframing, 20. *See also* Self-assessment
    thoughts about intellectual superiority, 32–33
    thoughts about rules, 17–18
    view of superiors, 22–24
Rehearsing scenarios, 26, 52, 119, 125. *See also* Role-play exercises
Reid (case study), 79–80, 87–90. *See also No Crying in Baseball*
Relational leader, 47
Relationship skills, 3. *See also* Intangible skill sets
    building, 108
    consequences from lack of, 96–97
    using goals to build, 92
Relentless, 67–70
Reliable, 146–54
Reluctance to act independently, 168
Reputation (your own). *See also* Perceptions (of you); Rebranding yourself;
        Self-assessment
    analyzing, 1–2
    benefits of analyzing, 6–8
    evaluating, 170–71
    hindrance, 162
    monitoring, 4
Requesting new assignments, 163
Resentment
    from peers, 38, 96–105
    of rules and authority, 17, 22

Reserved, 168
Resistance to authority, 15–19. *See also Don't Fence Me In*
Responsible, 140–41
Results, getting, 46
Risk-averse, 97–102, 105, 168
Risk-taking, importance of, 153
Robert, Henry Martyn (quoted), 105
Robotic, 80–85
Role model. *See* Mentor
Role-play exercises, 159. *See also* Rehearsing scenarios
Roosevelt, Eleanor (quoted), 90
Rules of the workplace. *See also* Authority
    adapting to changes in, 46–49
    taking exception to, 13–17

Safety Patrol. See also Paige (case study)
    applied self-awareness, 106–8
    five fast fixes, 103
    perception gap, 97–102
Seeking out new projects, 155
Self-assessment. *See also* Perceptions (of you); Reframing; Reputation
    Don't Fence Me In, 17, 18–19
    Dust in My Wind, 69, 72
    Faulty Volume Control, 113–18, 122–23
    Frozen Compass, 47–48
    Intellectual Snob, 32
    No Crying in Baseball, 83
    Passion Pistol, 134–35, 142
    Perpetual Doer, 150–51
    Safety Patrol, 99–100
    scale for rating perceptions, 173
    using past situations, 58, 61
    using personal attributes, 172f
Self-awareness. *See also* Applied self-awareness; Awareness of others; Emotional
        intelligence; Perceptions (of you)
    about, 3
    defined, 7, 173
    how to increase, 169–70
    manifesting, 75
    volume of one's self-promotion, 127
    while changing style of interacting, 48–51
Self-conscious, 109–10
Self-discipline, 41
Self-disclosure, 84–85, 86. *See also* Emotions, displaying
Self-importance. *See Intellectual Snob*
Self-promotion. *See* Volume (self-promotion)
Self-serving, 111–14
Selling out, 21–22
Shortcomings, admitting, 78
Shy, 168
Skeptical, 168
Small talk at work, 86
Smiling at work, 86
Snob. *See Intellectual Snob*

Visionary thinker, 160–61
Visual cues for changing behavior, 89, 93, 117
Volume (self-promotion). *See also Faulty Volume Control*
    too high, 116–18, 127–29, 137. *See also* Kyle (case study)
    too low, 114–16, 124–26. *See also* Graham (case study)
Volunteering, 71, 153
Vulnerability, showing, 89–90, 92. *See also* Emotions, displaying; Self-disclosure

Well-qualified, 30–35

Zealous. *See* Overzealous

CPSIA information can be obtained at www.ICGtesting.com
Printed in the USA
LVOW10s0521200813

348679LV00001B/55/P